HORSE
LAW

HORSE
LAW

Julie Mackenzie
of Lincoln's Inn, Barrister

J. A. Allen
London

To Woodspring Georgy

© Julie Mackenzie 2001
This edition first published in Great Britain 2001

Reprinted 2002

ISBN 0 85131 7820

J.A. Allen
Clerkenwell House
Clerkenwell Green,
London EC1R 0HT

J.A. Allen is an imprint of Robert Hale Ltd

British Library Cataloguing in Publication Data
A catalogue record for this book is available from the British Library

Design by Judy Linard
Illustrated by Maggie Raynor
Edited by Martin Diggle
Colour separation by Tenon & Polert Colour Scanning Ltd
Printed by Kyodo Printing Co(S'pore) Pte Ltd

CONTENTS

PUBLISHER'S NOTE

The law in the United Kingdom uses the male pronoun 'he' to refer to any person of either gender, and this convention has been followed in this book. However, except where they refer to a specific individual, the terms 'he' and 'his' may be taken as meaning 'he or she'; 'his or her' throughout.

PREFACE

It is eleven years since the first edition of this book appeared. Since then, the practice of the legal profession has changed considerably: in particular, there has been a move towards greater specialisation. This book was originally intended for the lay horse owner and as a starting point for the legal practitioner, and that intention remains, but it is not easy to cater for both readerships. For lay readers, the information must be comprehensible and not couched in overly legal language. However, the law is at times inevitably complex and there is a danger in over-simplification of becoming inaccurate. I trust, therefore, that my legal colleagues will forgive the explanation of legal terms, particularly Latin ones (some may be grateful for the latter!), and that the lay reader will appreciate the need for some legal language in order to ensure accuracy.

One of the most potentially fundamental changes to the law is the Human Rights Act 1998, which came into force on 2 October 2000. I have referred to this in the text, where I felt it relevant. The Act brings the European Convention on Human Rights into the law of the United Kingdom, so a claimant may now bring an action for breach of his human rights under the Act in the English Courts. There are likely to be areas, in particular of the criminal law, within our present legislation which will be affected because of incompatibility with the Convention. Where this occurs, the procedure is then to obtain a declaration of incompatibility from the High Court. This legislation has the potential to 'clog up' the system, but it will remain to be seen what the judiciary's view will be, and whether a robust view will be taken.

The Countryside and Rights of Way Act was given the Royal Assent on 30 November 2000, but only three sections came into force. More of the Act will have come into force on 30 January 2001, but for a substantial proportion of the Act, which contains potentially important changes, there is, at the time of writing, no commencement date. Where it is considered relevant, the Act has been referred to in Chapter 8.

There is, of course, no 'Horse Law' as such, and the law which can relate to horses covers many legal areas. Some of these are very specialised and I have referred to established works in some such areas.

I would also like to acknowledge the contributions of three of my colleagues: Ian Fenny of Guildhall Chambers, Bristol for Chapter 9 Road Traffic Law; Kerry Barker, also of Guildhall Chambers for Chapter 12 Betting and Gaming on Horses, and Charles Auld of St John's Chambers, Bristol for his assistance with Chapter 10 Keeping Horses.

Finally, the law does not stand still and, whilst every effort has been made to ensure that this book includes important recent decisions, inevitably there may be those that have not been included. This book relates to the law of England and Wales unless otherwise stated. The law is as at 18 January 2001.

Julie Mackenzie
Pump Court Chambers
London, Swindon and Winchester

January 2001

TABLE OF CASES

TABLE OF STATUTES

TABLE OF STATUTORY INSTRUMENTS

Chapter 1 OWNERSHIP

There are, in law, two classifications of animals: domestic and wild. These classifications are enshrined in English Common Law. Domestic animals are animals which are domestic or tame, whether by habit or training and live in association with man. Horses are considered domestic animals and this will include native horses and ponies that roam free on Britain's mountains and moorlands.

The horse's status as a domestic animal means that it is capable of being owned. Implicit in ownership are rights and an owner can maintain an action in the courts for detention (wrongful keeping of his horse). If a horse strays or is lost it still remains the owner's property. A foal, subject to any contrary agreement, is considered to be owned by its dam's owner.

The particular areas of ownership most likely to be of interest to horse owners are:

Theft
Conversion
Lending and borrowing
Protection

Theft

All animals which have value and are the property of any person can be subject to theft.

The law with regard to theft was rationalised by the Theft Act 1968. Theft is the dishonest appropriation (taking) of property belonging to another with the intention of permanently depriving the owner of that property (Theft Act 1968, s.1). The maximum term of imprisonment for theft on indictment is seven years.

A horse can be the subject of theft if it is taken from a person who has possession or control of it or who has a proprietory right or interest in the animal, although an equitable interest arising as a result of an agreement to create or transfer an interest is not sufficient. The animal must belong to someone before it can be stolen and in certain circumstances a person may not be guilty of theft if what is taken does not belong to anyone. However, whilst some property can be abandoned and, therefore, not belong to anyone, this is unlikely to be the case with a horse. If a seemingly abandoned horse is taken home by a well-meaning individual, looked after and efforts to trace the owner are made, then that person is unlikely to be charged with theft. Clearly, anyone who makes efforts to find the owner of a horse does not believe it was abandoned and the fact that efforts are made to establish ownership would indicate that there was no intention to permanently deprive an owner of his property.

If a horse can be stolen it follows that it can also be the subject of the offence of handling stolen goods (Theft Act 1968, s.22). It may be of some comfort to an owner whose horse is stolen to know that, if the horse is then purchased by someone, who knows or believes that the horse is stolen, that person has committed an offence.

A further offence under the Theft Act is obtaining by deception (s.15). If someone purchases a horse with a stolen cheque, then an offence has been committed.

All these offences can be tried either by the Magistrates' Court or the Crown Court, before a judge and jury.

A note of caution for an owner whose horse is stolen: it is an offence to advertise publicly a reward for the return of a horse, which is lost or stolen, using any words, the effect of which is, that no questions will be asked, or that any person returning the horse will be safe from enquiry or apprehension, or that any money that may have been paid to purchase the horse or advanced as a loan will be repaid (Theft Act 1968, ss.23, 34(2)(b)). The printer and publisher of such an advertisement will have committed an offence as well as the advertiser. This is triable by the Magistrates' Court and, on conviction, the penalty is a fine of up to £1,000.

Of course, if a horse is stolen, the owner's main concern is that it should be returned. Freeze marking is now widely available and can assist the police in their search for stolen animals. In addition, it affords some degree of protection against the horse being sold for meat. New methods of identifying horses are genetic profiling and microchipping, which also help if a horse is stolen. An increasing number of horses, particularly those used for breeding or competition, are now registered on the British Horse Database, and this is another source of protection for the horse owner.

Conversion

Conversion remains a complex area of the law despite attempts at simplification made by the Torts (Interference with Goods) Act 1977. However, it can be relevant to the horse owner and is, therefore, dealt with here as simply as possible.

Conversion, which is essentially the civil equivalent of certain crimes under the Theft Act, occurs where a person entitled to the possession of a chattel (i.e. a thing) is permanently deprived of that possession and it is 'converted' to someone else's use. Various acts, among which are wrongful taking of property, wrongly parting with property and wrongful retention of property, can constitute conversion.

Conversion by taking is taking possession, without authority, of another person's goods with the intention of asserting some right over them. An obvious example is someone taking a horse and riding it without the owner's knowledge or consent. The intention of the party taking the property does not have to be to acquire full ownership, although returning the horse might amount to mitigation of any damages claimed. The taker would, however, be liable for damages for any injury to the animal before it was returned, and possibly to compensate the owner for being deprived of the horse.

Wrongful parting with property will usually involve the purported transfer of some right over the property. It follows, therefore, that anyone trying to sell an animal, in which he does not possess any rights, will be liable in conversion and the owner of the animal will be entitled to sue for damages.

If an auctioneer, who may or may not be aware of the true ownership of a horse, nonetheless deals with a horse without the owner's consent or authority, he will be liable in conversion as against the owner. An auctioneer's liability is strict: he is liable to the true owner.

Conversion by keeping does not include simple keeping without permission. There must be some act or omission, which is inconsistent with the rights of the owner. This type of conversion might occur where the person having a horse in his possession refuses to give it up to the owner, or other person entitled to the animal, when asked. If, therefore, a person borrowing a horse refuses to return it to the owner on demand, the owner is entitled to sue for damages and also, perhaps more importantly, he can ask the court for an order that the horse be returned.

Lending and Borrowing Horses

When a horse is lent, be it to friend or to a stranger, in the absence of express terms to the contrary, the law will imply certain obligations upon both parties, on the basis of what is known as a contract of bailment. Bailment is the delivery of goods by one person (the bailor) to another (the bailee) for a limited purpose, upon the basis that the bailee will return the goods to the bailor, or deal with the goods as per the bailor's instructions after the purpose for which they were delivered has been fulfilled.

The borrower or bailee

Where the borrower has the horse for his use and, therefore, for his benefit rather than the lender's, he will be liable for the slightest act of negligence on his part, which means that he must exercise the utmost care not only of the horse, but also its equipment. Where, however, the borrower is simply keeping the horse for the owner, then because the owner is benefiting, a slightly lower standard of care is acceptable. It is, of course, open to the parties to draw up an agreement between them as to responsibilities. Where there is no agreement, then the borrower will be responsible for the cost of feeding, veterinary expenses and any damage caused to the horse whilst in his care, including damage by a third party.

A borrower is only entitled to use the horse for the purpose for which it is lent, which means, for example, that he should not hunt a horse lent as a companion. If the horse is injured when used for any purpose other than that for which it was lent, then the borrower will be liable in damages. If a bailee is so negligent that a borrowed horse is neglected or injured and has to be put down, this will also amount to conversion of the horse (see page 3). Any action by a bailee which is inconsistent with the terms of the bailment and in contravention of the bailor's (lender's) rights, will also be conversion.

The lender or bailor

When lending a horse, the lender must make the borrower aware of any defects which the horse may have, which are known to the lender. However, the lender need only disclose vices which would affect the purpose for which the animal is lent. Where a horse has not been used for some considerable time and is lent, the borrower must be informed. If the borrower is not informed, rides the animal and as a result is injured, he is entitled to sue the lender. The lender will not be liable for injuries caused by defects of which he is not aware; nor would a lender be liable to third parties in respect of injuries occasioned by the borrower's negligent use of the horse.

In the recent case of *Westphal and Barmer Ersatzkasse v Alexander* (2000) in the High Court the court considered the duty of care owed by a lender of a horse to the borrower, who was a friend. The borrower was unfortunately thrown from the horse and suffered serious injuries. It was held that the borrower's duty of care is that of the reasonable owner or rider. There is a duty upon the lender to assess the borrower's ability to ride and such assessment should be of the borrower's ability to walk, trot and canter safely. The judge also held that if the lender believes or suspects that the horse may behave in an unpredictable way, perhaps because it has not been ridden for a while, then the lender should inform the borrower. This case does not, however, suggest that the borrower should be treated as an expert (unless, presumably, the borrower holds himself out as such.) In this case, the judge found that:

(i) The lender's (defendant's) assessment was adequate.

(ii) As the lender had ridden the horse himself before the accident, he did not breach his duty of care by failing to warn the borrower that the horse had not been ridden for three months.

(iii) He could not be satisfied that, had the borrower been so advised, she would not have ridden the horse in any event.

This case enforces the need, not only for the lender to disclose all he knows about the horse, but also to make an assessment of the borrower.

As horses are often loaned it is sensible for there to be a written agreement as to the terms of the loan arrangement. Such terms should include the period of notice required for the return of the horse. Both parties should keep a copy. This should help to reduce the potential for litigation.

Protection

We have established that horses can be property under the definition of the Theft Act 1968, and they are also property as defined in The Criminal Damage Act 1971. Under s.1(1) of that Act it is an offence to destroy or damage any animal which belongs to another person, without lawful excuse, either intending to destroy or damage such property or being reckless as to whether property of another will be destroyed or damaged.

Thus, to constitute an offence under the Criminal Damage Act, the horse must belong to another person, and destroying or damaging horses which are in one's ownership does not constitute an offence under this Act. It may, however, give rise to an offence under the Protection of Animals Act 1911.

In establishing a case under the Criminal Damage Act, it is necessary to prove intention or recklessness. It is not necessary to prove that an instrument was used. Under s.3 it is an offence to have in one's custody or under one's control anything which one intends without lawful excuse to use to destroy or damage property.

Section 2(a) provides that any person who, without lawful excuse, makes to another a threat, intending that the other would fear it would be carried out, to destroy or damage any animal belonging to that person, commits an offence.

The Criminal Damage Act allows specifically for defences to offences under the Act.

First, if a defendant believes that at the time of the offence the person whom he believed to be entitled to consent to the destruction of or damage to the animal in question had so consented or would have so consented if he had known of it and its circumstances, this constitutes a defence. The belief must be honestly held and it is immaterial whether the belief is justified.

Second, it is a defence if the defendant acted in the way he did in order to protect property belonging to himself or another or to protect a right or interest, including sporting rights, in which he, or that other person, either possessed or he believed he possessed, and at the time of the offence also believed (i) that the property, right or interest was in immediate need of protection and (ii) that the means of protection used or proposed were or would be reasonable in all the circumstances.

In addition, an honest, even if unreasonable, belief that the animal belonged to the defendant would be a good defence. Equally, if the defendant caused the damage in self-defence he would be entitled to be acquitted.

Criminal damage is triable either by the Magistrates' Court or the Crown Court, save that, where the value of the property is less than £5,000 it must be tried summarily. Upon indictment, the maximum prison sentence is ten years and summarily the maximum sentence is three months or a fine or both.

Offences under sections 2 and 3 are triable either way and upon indictment the maximum term is ten years whilst summarily it is six months or a fine or both.

It is within the power of the Criminal Courts to make a compensation order where a person is convicted of an offence of destroying or damaging property, such property including animals. A compensation order may be in addition to, or instead of, any other penalty. Compensation must be of such an amount as the court considers appropriate, having regard to any evidence in relation to the amount and any representations either by the defendant or on behalf of the prosecution.

If an animal is shot, the shooter may be liable to a civil action for its value, unless he can show that he had no other means of protecting his property.

Where there is no justification, and the animal suffered, then as an alternative to a charge of criminal damage, there may be a charge of cruelty under the Protection of Animals Act.

Ownership of Straying Animals

One other aspect of the law which affects ownership is that which pertains to straying. The owner or keeper of a horse found straying on the highway commits an offence under the Highways Act 1980 and is liable to a fine not exceeding level 3 on the standard scale, which is presently £1,000. The Animals Act 1971 also impacts upon the issue of straying, see Straying in Chapter 3.

Chapter 2 NEGLIGENCE

The ownership of horses brings with it both the rights discussed in Chapter 1 and responsibilities. Most of these responsibilities fall within the law of negligence.

Negligence can arise in many situations, whether by direct act or omission. It is necessary, therefore, to cover it in some detail. A full discussion of the subject would take a whole book, for example *Charlesworth on Negligence*. Here it is intended to deal with the subject in a fairly simple form.

To begin with, let us consider the question: 'What is negligence?

> Negligence is the omission to do something which a reasonable man, guided upon those considerations which ordinarily regulate the conduct of human affairs, would do or doing something which a prudent and reasonable man would not do.

This definition, given by Baron Alderson in *Blyth v Birmingham Waterworks Co* (1856), was the first real judicial guidance in the concept of negligence. This definition, however, has been expanded and the nature of negligence now was formulated by Lord MacMillan in *Donaghue v Stevenson* [1932], when he stated that:

...the cardinal principle of liability is that the party complained of should owe the party complaining a duty to take care and that the party complaining should be able to prove that he has suffered damage in consequence of a breach of that duty.

Establishing Negligence

In order to establish negligence three factors have to be proved.

1. That there was a duty of care. Lord MacMillan stated in *Donaghue v Stevenson* [1932] that the categories of negligence are never closed. In considering whether a duty of care exists the court will consider:
    a) Whether the damage is foreseeable.
    b) Whether there is a relationship of proximity between the parties.
    c) Whether the imposition of such duty on the parties would be fair just and reasonable.
2. That there was a breach of that duty.
3. That as a result of that breach, damage was caused.

Unless all three can be proved, there can be no successful negligence action, and the burden of proving negligence generally rests upon the claimant. In some circumstances, however, the burden shifts to the defendant, namely where the claimant has proved injury resulting from behaviour which could only be reasonably explained by a breach of duty by the defendant. The defendant must then prove that he took all reasonable precautions to avoid the conduct complained of. The standard of proof is not as high as in a criminal case, being on a balance of probabilities rather than beyond reasonable doubt.

The duty to take care can mean a duty not to do something, or not to fail to do something, and whether the relevant act or omission amounts to negligence will depend on the facts of each case.

So far as the question of damages is concerned, the damage caused by the breach of duty must be damage that was reasonably foreseeable. In general, a defendant must take his victim as he finds him; it is no defence to say, for instance, that, if the claimant had not had a pre-existing condition, his injuries would not have been so serious.

General examples of duty of care

The acts or omissions which can give rise to a duty of care are many and varied and the boundaries are being gently expanded all the time. In relation to the equestrian world there are numerous examples, three of which would be:

1. In addition to his duties under the Sale of Goods Act, a saddler owes a duty to those who purchase goods from him, whether these are goods he has made himself or those that he is selling second hand.

2. Riding schools and instructors, whether employed or freelance, owe a duty of care to their clients or pupils and to their staff.

3. Organisers of competitions owe a duty of care to the competitors and spectators and competitors owe a duty of care to each other and to spectators.

The legal standard of care owed is an objective one; it is the standard of care which might be expected from a person of ordinary prudence or a person of ordinary care and skill. In some situations the court has recognised a distinction in certain fields between amateurs and professionals and, consequentially, in their levels of competence.

So far as children are concerned, a child has to attain the standard of care to be expected of a child of that age. Where a child is a claimant he is not expected to take the same degree of care as an adult. The standard of care required for a child from an adult will also be dictated by the child's age, as will the question of contributory negligence. See *McHale v Watson* [1966] 115 CLR 199 followed in *Mullin v Richard* [1998] 1All ER 920.

There may be certain circumstances where a parent will liable for the negligence of a child.

Proving Negligence

The burden of proof

The person who has to prove the negligence is the claimant. He must show that he was injured by a negligent act or omission for which, in law, the defendant is responsible. The claimant has to prove the three elements of a negligence claim:

1. That there was some duty owed by the defendant to the claimant.
2. That there was some breach of that duty.
3. That an injury was caused to the claimant which was as a result of the breach of duty.

The claimant has to prove the facts from which the court can properly infer that the injury was caused as a result of the defendant's negligence. It is not sufficient to prove facts which are equally consistent with the defendant's negligence or the claimant's. The cause of the damage must be certain.

Res ipsa loquitor

This means 'the facts speak for themselves'. Under this doctrine a claimant establishes a prima facie case of negligence if:

a) it is not possible for him to prove exactly what was the relevant act or omission which set in train the events which led to the accident and

b) on the evidence it would be more likely than not that the effective cause of the accident was some act or omission of the defendant.

There must be reasonable evidence of negligence. In other words, where the causes of an accident are unknown, but it could only have been caused by the defendant's negligence, the maxim applies. The defendant must be in control of the cause of the accident and this can include being in control of the defendant's employees. The accident itself must be one which would not ordinarily happen if proper care is taken.

The effect of the maxim *res ipsa loquitor* is to provide the court with evidence of negligence upon which the court is able to find for the claimant. It is open to the defendant to show that there was an accident, but it did not result from his negligence. In those circumstances he ousts the maxim and may not be liable. This does not change the burden of proof. If the defendant displaces the maxim then the court will look to the strength of the claimant's evidence to decide whether in fact the defendant is negligent.

Limitations of actions

The Limitation Act 1980, s.2, provides that actions for damages for negligence must be brought within six years from the date on which the cause of action occurred. Where, however, a claimant is seeking damages for personal injury, the limitation period is three years. The limitation period for bringing an action under the Fatal Accidents Acts 1976 is also three years, but the court does have the power to override this in certain circumstances.

Although the period of limitation usually begins to run from the date of the matter giving rise to the cause of action, in negligence actions the period of limitation runs from the date of damage occurring, rather than the date of the act causing the damage. Where personal injuries are involved, the limitation period runs from the date of the claimant's knowledge of the injury if that date is later than the date on which the cause of action began.

Defences – Limitation and Apportionment of Liability

Even where all three elements necessary to establish a claim can be proved, there can be defences to negligence. Liability can also be limited in certain circumstances, and liability may be apportioned.

Consent or *volenti non fit injuria*

Where a claimant relies upon the breach of duty to take care, if the claimant consented to that breach of duty or knew of the breach of duty and voluntarily incurred the whole risk of that breach, then a defence is established. For the defence to be successful the claimant must be shown to have realised the danger, appreciated it fully and voluntarily accepted the risk of it.

Whether the claimant's acceptance of the risk was voluntary is likely to be a question of fact and the court will be entitled to infer such acceptance from the claimant's conduct. Such inference is more likely to be drawn where it can be shown that the danger was apparent to the claimant and there was nothing to say that he was obliged to incur the danger, than in the situation where the claimant knew he was in danger but did not fully comprehend its extent, or where he had no opportunity of deciding whether he would accept the risk.

Volenti as a defence is unlikely to succeed where the relationship of employer and employee exists (although it is available in theory) because, if an employee is acting under a compulsion of duty to an employer, an acceptance of risk is unlikely to be inferred.

This defence is of particular relevance to persons competing with their horses or ponies. Riding or driving horses is a risk sport. Competitors take on the risk incidental to the sport and the competition and, therefore, cannot sustain an action for any injuries received in the course of the competition unless they are caused by some act or foul play which amounts to negligence (see *Reid v Mitchell* (1885) 22 Sc LR 748).

Spectators may recover damages in respect of an injury resulting from a negligent act of a participant or an omission by the organisers to prevent accidents which are foreseeable and not inherent in the sport. If it can be shown that the spectator agreed to take the risk of being injured by such negligence then the defence of *volenti* will apply.

Agreements to exclude or restrict liability

Despite its title, the Unfair Contract Terms Act 1977 applies to liability for negligence, in certain circumstances. These circumstances are breaches of:

1. Any obligation, arising from the express or implied terms of a contract, to take reasonable care or exercise reasonable skill in the performance of a contract.

2. Any common law duty to take reasonable care or exercise reasonable skill (but not any stricter duty).
3. The common duty of care imposed by the Occupier's Liability Act 1957.

The negligence must arise from things done by a person in the course of a business, or from the occupation of premises used for the business purposes of the occupier. The Act prevents a relevant person from raising the defence that he excluded or limited the liability for negligence by a term in the contract or by a notice, unless the term of notice was reasonable, and did not attempt to exclude or limit liability for death or personal injury. It is for those claiming that a contract term is reasonable to show that the term is reasonable.

The Unfair Contract Terms Act does not abolish the defence of *volenti non fit injuria*. Where a contract term purports to exclude or restrict liability for negligence, a person's agreement to or awareness of the risk is not, of itself, to be taken as showing his voluntary acceptance of the risk.

Contributory negligence

The Law Reform (Contributory Negligence) Act 1945 s.3(1) provides that where any person suffers damage as a result partly of his own fault and partly the fault of any other person or persons, a claim in respect of that damage is not to be defeated by reason of the fault of the person suffering the damage. The damages recoverable in respect thereof will be reduced to such extent as the court thinks just and equitable having regard to the claimant's share in the responsibility for the damage. This section sets out the basis for what is known as contributory negligence. This also applies where a person has died partly as a result of his own fault, and any damages recovered under the Fatal Accidents Act 1976 will be reduced in proportion.

In order to establish contributory negligence the defendant has to prove that the claimant was negligent, and his negligence was a cause of, or contributed to, the harm suffered by him. The negligence in this context is the claimant's failure to take reasonable care of himself, and this lack of care contributed to the injury suffered. In other words, had the claimant done or not done something that he reasonably should have not done or done, his injuries would not have been so serious, or would not have occurred at all. Where there is contributory negligence, the damages recoverable by the claimant will be reduced, on such a basis as the court sees fit, taking into account the claimant's share of responsibility. It is possible for a claimant to be considered 100 per cent contributory negligent.

The standard of care is what is reasonable in the circumstances. This usually responds to the standard of care in negligence, which depends upon foreseeability. This foreseeability is of the harm to oneself, and if a claimant ought reasonably to have foreseen that if he did not act as a reasonably prudent person, he might hurt himself, he is guilty of contributory negligence.

A claimant must take into account the possibility of others being careless. The claimant must exercise the standard of care expected of a person of normal intelligence and skill in the circumstances. The exception to this is that a child is only expected to show that degree of care reasonable to a child of his age.

It would be an instance of contributory negligence if a rider sustained a head injury when not wearing a riding hat, and it might well be argued successfully that not wearing a hat to an approved standard is also contributory negligence. A claimant's knowledge of existing danger is an important factor in establishing contributory negligence. The crucial point is not simply whether the claimant realised the danger, but whether the facts as he knew them would have caused a reasonable person in his position to recognise the danger. The test here is one of plain common sense: did the claimant contribute to the damage?

Joint tortfeasors (third party negligence)

Proving that the negligence of a third party contributed to the claimant's injury is not a defence. If a claimant sues two or more defendants successfully, in theory, he may be entitled to the full amount of his damages from each party. The usual practice, however, is for the court to exercise its power to apportion the damages as between the defendants.

The Law of Negligence and Horse Owners

Riding establishments

The proprietor of a riding establishment clearly owes a duty of care to his clients. This duty extends to clients who are visitors under the Occupier's Liability Acts, and the common law duties which a proprietor has to ensure that the client is as safe as reasonably practicable bearing in mind that riding is a risk sport.

Occupier's Liability Acts 1957 and 1984

These Acts regulate the duty of an occupier to his visitors in respect of any dangers due to the state of the premises or to things done or not done on the premises.

An 'occupier' does not have to have exclusive occupation: the test is whether a person has some degree of control of the premises, either as a result of his presence there, or the activities he carries out there.

A 'visitor' under the Act is anyone who is invited by the occupier or who is given permission to enter or use the premises. Clients of a riding establishment must, in this context, be visitors and any persons entering or using the premises under a contract will also be owed a common duty of care under the Occupier's Liability Act 1957 s.5(1).

The duty of care is to take such reasonable care as to ensure that the visitor will be reasonably safe in using the premises for the purpose for which he is entitled to be there. A warning by an occupier of any danger will not absolve the occupier from liability unless, in the circumstances, it was enough to enable the visitor to be reasonable safe (Occupier's Liability Act 1957, s.2(4)(a)).

The 1957 Act only covers lawful visitors to the premises. The duty of an occupier to trespassers was governed by common law rules until the Occupier's Liability Act 1984 was enacted. Under s.1(3) of the 1984 Act, the occupier will owe a duty to trespassers and other non-visitors if he is aware of a danger or has reasonable grounds to believe that the non-visitors are in the vicinity 'of the danger, whether or not they have lawful authority for being there', and the risk is one which in all the circumstances the occupier could be reasonably expected to protect those people from.

As with all areas of negligence, the standard of care owed to children will be higher because children cannot be expected to take the same care of themselves as would an adult. (See *Jolley v Sutton LBC* (2000) *The Times* 24 May ML.) This higher duty is of particular importance to persons running riding establishments where the majority of their clients are likely to be children.

Common law duty of care
The proprietor

The primary duty of care imposed on a riding establishment proprietor is to take care that the horse provided for the rider is suitable for the rider's ability. In order to do that, the proprietor must make reasonable enquiry of the rider's ability. Where such enquiry is not made and an unsuitable horse is provided, and the rider suffers injury, then a claim for negligence is likely to succeed. If, however, the rider on being asked does not give a true assessment of his ability, then an action is unlikely to arise, unless the horse was one which no 'amateur' experienced rider should have been asked to ride, without being warned of the nature of the animal.

Proprietors also have a duty to exercise care in what they allow clients to do. An extreme example would be allowing a complete beginner to ride around a cross-country course. However, the proprietor must take care that a pupil is not asked to do something which is quite clearly beyond his capabilities. In referring to 'the proprietor' it must be remembered that the proprietor will be vicariously liable for the negligent acts of his employees, provided that they are acting in the course of their employment.

Apart from taking reasonable care to provide a suitable horse, there is also a duty to ensure that the tack used is in good condition, fits correctly and is suitable for the particular horse.

The proprietor must provide a safe area in which to conduct lessons. A duty to provide a safe system of work falls upon an employer in respect of employees.

The proprietor's duties do not end at the riding establishment's gates and, where supervised rides are taken out, there must be proper supervision. Sufficient instruction should be given to anyone who has not ridden before or who is very inexperienced before they are allowed out on a ride. Also, the route of the ride must be compatible with the riders' capabilities.

In assessing the acts or omissions of a riding school proprietor, failure to follow the Code of Conduct set down by the British Horse Society for Approved Establishments may be considered as evidence of negligence. This may also apply to codes and standards set by the Association of British Riding Schools.

The rider
So far as the rider is concerned, he must take reasonable care of himself. In particular, he should always wear a proper riding hat and suitable shoes or boots. The various riding disciplines and the British Horse Society and the Association of British Riding Schools now set out specific standards for riding hats and these standards apply in riding schools. In addition, the Highway Code paragraph 34 refers to safety equipment, in particular that, under the Horses (Protective Headgear for Young Riders) Regulations 1992, children under the age of fourteen must wear a riding hat which complies with the regulations and it must be fastened securely. The code also recommends that other riders should do the same. As already suggested, the wearing of the incorrect standard of hat may give rise to a successful argument of contributory negligence, if it can be shown that an injury would not have occurred or not been so severe if the correct hat had been worn.

On the road
Road users, whether with horses or in cars, owe a duty of care to other road users. The Highway Code now provides increased guidance for drivers meeting horses. There is a general provision at paragraph 190 namely:

> When passing animals, drive slowly and be ready to stop. Do not scare animals by sounding your horn or revving your engine. Look out for animals being led or ridden on the road and take extra care and keep your speed down at left hand bends and on narrow country roads. If a road is blocked by a herd of animals, stop and switch off your engine until they have left the road. Watch out for animals on unfenced roads.

Paragraph 191 refers specifically to horse riders:

> Be particularly careful of horses and riders, especially when overtaking. Always pass wide and slow. Horse riders are often children, so take extra care and remember riders may ride in double file when escorting a young or inexperienced horse rider. Look out for horse rider's signals and heed a request to slow down or stop. Treat all horses as a potential hazard and take great care.

Paragraph 139 states that horse riders should be given at least as much room as you would a car when overtaking. In applying this part of the Highway Code it has been held that, where a driver meets a horse being ridden on a narrow road, he should exercise great caution when passing the horse, and it is his duty to slow down and give the horse a wide berth. If giving the horse a wide berth is not practical because there is another vehicle approaching from the other direction, then the driver should stop and wait before attempting to pass the horse (*Burns v Ellicott* (1969); *Carryfast v Hack* [1981]).

The Highway Code also sets out guidance for horse riders. This is found in paragraphs 35–41.

Paragraph 35 refers to clothing other than headgear. It recommends wearing boots and shoes with hard soles and heels, light coloured or fluorescent clothing in daylight and reflective clothing if you have to ride at night or in poor visibility.

Paragraph 36 recommends that it is safer not to ride on the road at night or in poor visibility, but if you do, make sure that your horse has reflective bands above the fetlock joints. Carry a light which shows white to the front and red to the rear.

Under paragraph 37, before you take a horse on to a road, you should:

a) ensure all tack fits well and is in good condition;

b) make sure you can control the horse.

You should always ride with other, less nervous horses if you think that your horse will be nervous of traffic, and never ride any horse on the road without a saddle or bridle.

Paragraph 38 states that, before riding off or turning, you should look behind you to make sure it is safe, then give a clear arm signal.

Paragraph 39 sets out some important guidance, namely:

(i)   Keep to the left.

(ii) Keep both hands on the reins unless you are signalling.

(iii) Keep both feet in the stirrups.

(iv) Do not carry another person.

(v)   Do not carry anything which might affect your balance or get tangled up with the reins.

(vi) Keep a horse you are leading to your left.

(vii) Move in direction of the traffic flow in a one way street.

(viii)Never ride more than two abreast, ride in single file where the road narrows or on the approach to a bend.

Paragraph 40 is a prohibition upon riding horses on footpaths, pavements or cycle tracks.

Paragraph 41 suggests avoiding roundabouts wherever possible. If it is necessary to use a roundabout then:

(i)   Keep to the left and watch out for vehicles crossing your path to leave or join the roundabout.

(ii) Signal right when riding across exits to show you are not leaving

(iii) Signal left just before you leave the roundabout.

Although a failure to observe the provisions of the Highway Code does not of itself render a person liable to criminal proceedings of any kind, any such failure may, in any proceedings (whether civil or criminal including offences under the Road Traffic Acts) be relied upon by any party to proceedings as tending to establish or negate any liability which is in question in those proceedings (Road Traffic Act 1998).

If these provisions of the Highway Code are not followed, there-fore, this can support a case of negligence by a rider as well as by the driver of a car. It may also give rise to contributory negligence.

The duty upon a rider is to use reasonable care and, as with a driver (*Nettleship v Weston* [1971]), this means, in this context, the skill and care that an experienced and competent rider would exer-cise. There are no variations in this standard of skill and it is not open to a rider to claim that he is only a novice.

It is not surprising that there are a number of decisions relating to horses on the road. The cases tend to confirm that a high standard of care is expected of persons riding or in control of horses on the road. It has been held that the pulling of the wrong rein can be evidence of negligence (*Wakeman v Robinson* (1823)), as has the spurring of a horse when it was close enough to a passer-by to kick out at him (*North v Smith* (1861)).

It is, perhaps, of some comfort to the rider that he cannot be expected to guard against dangers which could not have been foreseen. In *Hammack v White* (1862) the defendant was trying out a new horse in Finsbury Circus, which even then was a busy thoroughfare. Without warning and for no apparent reason the horse became difficult, the rider was unable to control it and it mounted the pavement and caused the claimant's husband serious injuries, from which he died. The claimant was unable to prove negligence because the defendant had done all that could be expected of a competent and skilful rider in an effort to control the horse.

The question raised in *Cutler v United Dairies*(London) Ltd [1933] was whether a horse owner is in breach of his duty of care if he has knowledge of the horse's propensities, but still allows him out on the road. It is a question of degree. Lord Justice Scrutton was caused some concern by the suggestion that, if a horse had once shied and the owner knew it had, then the owner would be responsible for any damage the horse might do in the future by shying. Fortunately, the learned Lord Justice took the view that shying, and knowledge thereof, was not sufficient to render the rider liable. He further took the view that shying was an ordinary habit, saying, 'I cannot believe that there is any horse in England which has not at some time or other shied at something. I cannot believe that it is not the ordinary habit of horses being nervous animals to shy frequently at sights or noises to which they are unaccustomed.'

The question of shying was raised in *Haines v Weston* [1981], although *Cutler v United Dairies* [1933] was not cited. The Court of Appeal did, however, take a similar view to that expressed by Scrutton LJ in *Cutler v United Dairies*. In *Haines v Weston*, the plaintiff was riding his horse along a country road on the left hand side. The defendant was driving his motor car in the same direction along the road and the defendant collided with the horse. The plaintiff claimed against the defendant in respect of damages for injury and loss, and the defendant counterclaimed. The plaintiff's claim was settled and a trial held on the counterclaim. The main allegation of negligence by the defendant was that the claimant had caused, permitted or allowed his horse to move to the right as the defendant was about to overtake him. The claimant, in giving evidence, said that the horse had shied and that he had temporarily lost control of it. The judge took the view that, in taking the horse upon the highway and knowing that there were things in the hedgerow which might frighten the horse, the claimant was under a duty to control the horse so that it would not move sideways if startled. The rider had not been able to control the horse and was therefore liable. The claimant appealed. It was held that the judge was in fact imposing an absolute duty upon a rider of a horse ridden properly on the highway to prevent it going out of control, and O'Connor LJ was quite satisfied that that proposition did not represent the law. Anyone seeking to succeed in an action for damages for injury by a horse must prove negligence. The fact that the horse had suddenly moved into the defendant's path called for an explanation by the claimant and the explanation given by the claimant was sufficient to negate any inference of negligence which might have been drawn from the actions of the horse.

Claims between riders

Claims also arise between riders of horses and in an unreported case, *Poynter v Beech Equestrian Centre and Diana, Duchess of Norfolk*, the claimant was out riding with the second defendant when the second defendant's horse kicked the claimant. The claimant sued under the Animals Act 1971, on the basis that the horse was known to be of a vicious and mean disposition, and in negligence, claiming that the second defendant (i) was riding too close to the claimant, and (ii) failed to control her horse properly. The claim under the Animals Act failed, but on the facts the judge decided that the second defendant was liable. The first defendant was not sued in negligence. This is a somewhat unusual decision, particularly in the light of *Breedon v Lampard* (1985), another unreported case, in the Court of Appeal. That case involved a claim for damages arising out of a riding accident which occurred at a cubbing meet of the Atherstone Hunt. Both parties were out with the field and were experienced horsewomen.

Mrs Lampard, 'the respondent' had placed a red velvet square on the horse's tail, not because she had known the horse to kick, but to warn people this was a young horse, so that they would keep away from it. The respondent was at the rear of the field when the hunt changed direction and a number of the members of the hunt passed the respondent. The respondent, with other followers, including the appellant, turned to follow. The appellant was close behind the respondent's horse 'Raffles' who shuffled to the left and kicked out, as a result of which the appellant suffered a broken leg. As in the previous case, the claim was brought under the Animals Act 1971 and in negligence. The judge at first instance found there was no breach of the Animals Act, nor was the respondent negligent. On appeal, the judge's findings were upheld. Their Lordships had little difficulty with the question of negligence, but the Animals Act point was considered more fully (see Chapter 3). What these two cases demonstrate is that whether or not a person is negligent when riding will, to an extent, be governed by the facts of the particular case.

It would, however, appear that where a horse displays a known vice of some seriousness and despite that knowledge, the owner or rider does not take precautions consistent with that knowledge, then any damage caused by the horse may give rise to claim in negligence. Where, however, a normally quiet, well-behaved horse acts uncharacteristically and causes damage then, generally speaking, no action in negligence will arise. Nevertheless, the bolting of a horse, which has been left unattended in a public street, is prima facie evidence of the negligence of its owner (*Gayler and Pope Ltd v B Davies and Son Ltd* [1924] 2 KB 75).

Horse owners and riders should particularly be aware that a higher standard of care is owed to children than to adults. This is especially relevant as horses hold considerable allure for children.

The *novus actus* intervention of a third party does not usually render the horseman liable. In other words, if an incident occurs because a third party intervenes, then the horseman will not necessarily be liable. If, however, the possibility of such intervention could have been foreseen and no reasonable action was taken by the rider, then he may be liable for damage caused by that third party. (*Haynes v Harwood* [1934]).

Sporting Activities

Sporting activities are another area where potentially the rider may fall foul of the law of negligence. There is ample scope because any sporting event has organisers who may owe a duty of care to the competitors and to the spectators. Equally the competitors owe a duty to the spectators, as well as to each other.

Competitors

The general principle is that the competitor voluntarily takes the risks that occur in the lawful pursuit of the particular sport. This principle is based on the doctrine of *volenti non fit injuria*, which has been discussed earlier. A rider who has knowledge of the risks, but still enters into a dangerous situation, is said to be voluntarily taking the risk. When sportsmen participate, the law assumes that they are aware of the risks incidental to the particular sport. This assumption, however, only extends to the risks which are foreseeable. When a competitor acts outside the scope of the sport and a fellow competitor is injured, then a claim for damages may be made.

Organisers owe a duty to competitors taking part in a competition organised by them. This duty is not intended to protect the competitors from the ordinary risks of the particular sport, but they do have a duty to ensure that there are no avoidable outside factors which could cause damage. A rider could clearly sue the organisers of a showjumping competition who placed the jumps in an area full of molehills if the rider or, indeed, the horse was injured as a result. The competitor does not take on additional risks which are products of the unsuitable nature of the premises (*Giles v London County Council* (1903)).

Spectators

Spectators are owed a duty of care by both competitors and organisers of sporting events and, if either are negligent, then the spectator can recover damages for injuries sustained. The question is, what constitutes negligence?

The leading case in respect of horse owners is *Wooldridge v Sumner* [1962]. In that case a competitor, who was very experienced, was showing a heavy hunter, which was subsequently judged Supreme Champion. Whilst showing the horse, the rider was endeavouring to do so to its best advantage in order to win the competition. Two feet away from the edge of the competition area there were a number of tubs, behind which was a cinder track surrounding the arena. Whilst galloping, as required, the horse went into and behind the line of tubs where the claimant, a film cameraman, was standing and the claimant was injured. The claimant had been warned by a steward to remain outside the competition area while the horses were galloping. The claimant brought an action against the owner of the horse and, at first instance, it was found that the rider had brought the horse into the corner much too fast and that, when it crashed into the tubs, it would have gone onto the cinder track, avoiding the claimant, if the rider had allowed it to do so. The claimant was awarded damages, and the defendant appealed. On appeal, the court held that negligence had not been established, first, because on the facts, any excessive speed around the corner was not the cause of the accident and was not negligence, but merely an error of judgement. Second, the finding that the horse would have gone onto the cinder track if its rider had allowed it, was an inference that was unjustified and in any event it did not amount to negligence.

In *Wooldridge v Sumner* Diplock LJ stated the principle in these terms:

> A person, attending a game or competition, takes the risk of any damage caused to him by an act of a participant done in the course of and for the purpose of the game or competition, notwithstanding, that such act may have involved an error of judgement or a lapse of skill, unless the participant's conduct is such as to evince a reckless disregard of the spectator's safety.

This case does not, however, allow the competitor to disregard completely the risk his action may have upon the spectator. In a subsequent case, *Wilks v Cheltenham Car Club* (1971), in which *Wooldridge v Sumner* was considered, it was held that a competitor in a race, going all out to win, owed a duty to spectators not to show reckless disregard for their safety, nor to cause injury by error of judgement, which a reasonable competitor would not have made and which could not, in the stress of circumstances, be regarded as excusable.

Organisers

The liability of the organisers to both competitors and spectators may arise under the Occupier's Liability Acts or in negligence or sometimes in both. A contract may also give rise to a duty of care under the Occupier's Liability Act 1957(s.5(1)). In general, organisers of an event, if not normally occupiers of the land upon which the event is held, will be occupiers for the purpose of the event and, as such, owe a duty of care to the competitors and spectators. In the case of *Wooldridge v Sumner* (above), there was also a claim against the British Horse Society as organisers of the show and occupiers of the stadium for the duration of the show. This claim was, however, dismissed as the duty of the British Horse Society to take all reasonable safety precautions had not been breached. Thus the organisers must be in breach of their duty to take all reasonable precautions to ensure the safety of competitors and spectators before a claim will be successful.

Where a person is injured, but there is no negligence on the part of the organisers, they cannot be held liable (*Hall v Brooklands Racing Club* [1932]). However, it is clearly incumbent upon the organisers of equestrian events to ensure that every reasonable precaution in respect of safety for competitors and spectators must be taken.

It is important that organisers are also aware of their contractual duty to competitors. When a competitor enters a competition he enters into a contract with the organisers. Disclaimers are almost always seen on a schedule for competitions. In circumstances where the organisers run an equestrian centre, this a business and any exclusion clauses will be covered by the Unfair Contract Terms Act 1977. In other circumstances, organisers must be aware that, in order to rely upon an exclusion clause which seeks to exclude liability for negligence, they must ensure that it is incorporated as a term of the contract between them and the competitors. This means that reasonable steps must be taken to bring it to the competitors' notice. It is not sufficient to just put it at the bottom of the schedule. In addition, the terms of the clause must be clear and unambiguous.

Statements

It was established in *Hedley Byrne v Heller* [1964] that where a defendant, who carries on a business and holds himself out as having some skill or qualification, makes a statement, which is relied upon by the plaintiff and this statement is negligently given, the defendant may be liable.

This principle is of particular interest to persons purchasing a horse. Clearly, if an expert who is expressly asked to give an opinion is negligent and is relied upon, then the expert can be sued if the advice was negligently given. Indeed, even a friend giving a negligent opinion which is relied upon may be successfully sued (*Chaudhry v Prabhakar* [1988]).

Equally, if a veterinary surgeon is requested to examine a horse before purchase and is negligent in that examination, then the purchaser may sue the veterinary surgeon if he suffers loss as a result of that negligence.

As with any other person holding themselves out as an expert or the member of a profession, a veterinary surgeon is expected to exercise the ordinary standard of skill which is to be expected from a member of that profession. If he falls below that standard and loss is suffered he may be sued. He is also vicariously liable for his assistant. (For further information on the veterinary profession, see Veterinary Surgeons, Chapter 11.)

Nuisance

Although, from a lawyer's point of view, nuisance is a separate cause of action from negligence, it is included in this chapter because, from a layman's point of view, the two are sometimes indistinguishable. Indeed, even lawyers have admitted an overlap. In *Goldman v Hargrave* [1967] Lord Wilberforce said '...nuisance, uncertain in its boundary, may comprise a wide variety of situations, in some of which negligence plays no part, in others of which it is decisive'.

Nuisance divides into public nuisance (which is also a criminal offence), private nuisance and statutory nuisance.

Public nuisance is, in simple terms, the unlawful doing of an act (or failure to do an act) which endangers the comfort, health, lives, property or safety of the public. It is not necessary for the whole public to be affected, provided a large section of it is. Public nuisance is only actionable as a civil wrong when a private individual has suffered particular damage above and beyond that suffered by the public.

The Environmental Protection Act 1990 creates certain statutory nuisances. These are to be found in Part III of the Act and are:

a) any premises in such a state as to be prejudicial to health or a nuisance,

b) smoke emitted from premises so as to be prejudicial to health or a nuisance,

c) any fumes or gases emitted from premises so as to be prejudicial to health or a nuisance,

d) any dust, steam, smell or other effluvia arising on industrial, trade or business premises and being prejudicial to health or a nuisance,

e) any accumulation or deposit which is prejudicial to health or is a nuisance,

f) any animal kept in such a place or manner as to be prejudicial to health or a nuisance,

g) noise emitted from premises so as to be prejudicial to health or a nuisance,

h) noise that is prejudicial to health or a nuisance and is emitted from or caused by a vehicle, machinery or equipment in a street,

i) any other matter declared by enactment to be a statutory nuisance.

The defendant in an action for private nuisance, on the other hand, has often not done anything unlawful *per se* (of itself). The action only arises if what he is doing adversely affects the land of his neighbour whether by causing an encroachment upon it, causing physical damage to it or by significant interference with the neighbour's enjoyment of it. In deciding whether a nuisance has been committed, the court will, amongst other things, consider the character of the neighbourhood. To quote the famous statement of

Thesiger LJ (at page 856) in *Sturges v Bridgeman* (1879):

> ...whether anything is a nuisance or not is a question to be determined, not merely by an abstract consideration of the thing itself, but in reference to its circumstances: what would be a nuisance in Belgrave Square would not necessarily be so in Bermondsey; and where a locality is devoted to a local trade or manufacture carried on by the traders or manufacturers in a particular and established manner not constituting a public nuisance, judges and juries would be justified in finding...that the trade or manufacture so carried on in that locality is not a private or actionable wrong.

The keeping of horses in a country area should not, therefore, of itself cause a nuisance. In the light of the Environmental Protection Act 1990, however, more particular care needs to be taken by horse owners to ensure that their premises do not emit unpleasant odours, etc. which could constitute a nuisance. This is particularly relevant for those running equestrian businesses. It should be noted that there are decided cases which have held that stables themselves can, in law, be a nuisance (*Rapier v London Tramways Co* [1893]), as can a manure works (*Knight v Gardner* (1869)) and, in certain circumstances, manure heaps (*Milner v Spencer* (1976)).

There are various other subsidiary matters of which horse keepers should be mindful. For example, barbed wire is a potential nuisance as well as having the potential to give rise to an action for negligence. An occupier of land owes a duty of care and although he may make use of barbed wire on his land, if the barbed wire is so placed on land adjoining a highway, that it is likely to be injurious to persons or animals lawfully using the highway, it is a nuisance which the local authority may serve notice upon the occupier to remove under the Highways Act 1980 s.164. If the occupier fails to comply with the notice the Magistrates' Courts may require him to abate (in this context remove) the nuisance. In this respect, horse keepers are advised to be mindful of the general definition of public nuisance given above, when carrying out any act which may have an impact upon members of the public.

Chapter 3 THE ANIMALS ACT 1971

The Animals Act 1971 clarifies certain areas of liability in respect of animals, known as strict liability. The essence of strict liability is that negligence does not have to be proved. Horses are covered by the Act, which deals with certain injuries that they may cause as well as any damage which may arise from straying.

Non-dangerous Species

Section 2(1) of the Act states that: 'Where damage is caused by an animal which does not belong to a dangerous species, a keeper of the animal is liable for damage, except as otherwise provided by this Act, if
a) the damage is of a kind which the animal, unless restrained, was likely to cause or which, if caused by the animal, was likely to be severe; and
b) the likelihood of the damage or of its being severe was due to the

characteristics of the animal, which are not normally found in animals of the same species or are not normally so found except at particular times or in particular circumstances; and

c) these characteristics were known to the keeper or were at any time known to a person, who at that time had charge of the animal as the keeper's servant or, where that keeper is the head of a household, were known to another keeper of the animal, who is a member of that household and under the age of sixteen.'

'Keeper' is defined in s.6(3) as someone who:

(i) owns the animal or has it in his possession, or

(ii) is head of a household, where a member of that household is under sixteen and owns the animal or has it in his possession.

In a recent decision it was held that there was nothing in the Act to prevent a keeper within the meaning of section 6(3) from relying upon section 2 to sue another person who was also the keeper of the same animal. (*Flack v Hudson and Another, The Times* 22 November 2000.) This is an important decision. It was argued that one keeper could not sue another under the Act as their knowledge of the characteristics of the animal would be the same. Lord Justice Otton did not accept the argument and held that, at common law, a bailor (i.e. someone who had borrowed the horse) had a clear and established right of action and there was nothing in the 1971 Act to limit who could bring an action in these circumstances.

Section 6(4), however, relieves the temporary keeper of a horse from liability where the horse has been taken into and kept in possession in order to prevent it from causing danger or to return it to its owner. The wording of this section does, however, mean that, where a horse is left with a trainer or at livery and it causes injuries, the owner as well as the trainer or proprietor can be liable. This is by virtue of the owner's ownership and the trainer's possession.

The phrase 'head of the household' is also likely to cause difficulties as the tradition of the male head of the family has been eroded. With whom will liability lie in the case of an extended family unit, perhaps including grandparents or aunts or uncles, or indeed two sisters running a household? These will be questions of fact for the court to decide.

There are defences to section 2 of the Act, which are contained in section 5, namely:
(i) where the claimant is at fault;
(ii) where the claimant voluntarily accepts the risk; or
(iii) where the claimant was trespassing.

The defence of voluntarily accepting the risk is the same as the principle of *volenti non fit injuria* in negligence (see Chapter 2). In other words, the claimant must be aware of the risk and continue to act despite that risk. This defence may not, however, necessarily apply where the claimant is a servant. Section 6(5) provides 'Where a person employed as a servant by a keeper of an animal incurs a risk incidental to his employment, he shall not be treated as accepting it voluntarily' (s.5(3)(a)). The vital words here are 'incidental to his employment'. However, it may be that the claimant was guilty of some degree of fault or contributory negligence, or that the risk taken was not incidental to his employment.

Where a claimant is trespassing, the defendant will not be liable provided:
(i) that the animal was not kept on the property for the protection of persons on the property, or
(ii) if it was kept for protection purposes, that keeping it for that purpose was not unreasonable(s.5(3)(b)).

This section really applies to dogs, as horses are not generally used for protecting premises. A keeper will not be liable if the damage caused is due wholly to the fault of the person suffering it (s.5(1)).

In order for a person injured to succeed in his claim, he must prove that the damage occurred and that:
(i) any damage caused was severe, and
(ii) the horse had abnormal characteristics, and
(iii) the horse's keeper knew of these characteristics, his knowledge being either actual or constructive.

Abnormal Characteristics

Abnormal characteristics must be those which are not usually found in horses. In *Wallace v Newton* [1982] the claimant was a groom at the defendant's training stables. Whilst attempting to lead a thoroughbred showjumper, with the appropriate name of 'Lord Justice', into a trailer, the claimant was crushed and seriously injured when the horse became violent or unreasonable. As the claimant's injuries were as a result of the horse's characteristics of unpredictability and unreliability, both of which are unusual in a horse, the claimant satisfied that limb of her claim. It was held that unpredictability is not a normal characteristic in a horse and it was not necessary for the plaintiff to prove that the animal concerned had any vicious tendency.

In the unreported case of *Breedon v Lampard* (1985), their Lordships upheld the trial judge's finding that there was no claim under the Animals Act 1971, but, whilst discussing briefly the claim in negligence, the Animals Act claim was dealt with more fully. The judge at first instance found that the damage was not of a kind which the animal was likely to cause and had he been deciding that, Sir George Waller said he would have agreed with that finding.

In respect of s.5(1)(b), it was argued that this case fitted within the definition of that clause. Sir George Waller found that:

> There were no characteristics of this animal to which the likelihood of damage being severe could be due, nor if it were relevant, to which the likelihood of damage could be due. There were no characteristics which are not normally found in animals of the same species.

Lloyd LJ was of the same opinion, saying:

> The essential condition for liability now is that the characteristic which is known to the owner must be a characteristic which is abnormal for the species... if liability is based on the possession of some abnormal characteristic known to the owner, then I cannot see any sense in imposing liability when the animal is behaving in a perfectly normal way for all animals of that species in these circumstances, even though it would not be normal for these animals to behave in that way in other circumstances.

His Lordship found it difficult to believe that parliament intended to impose liability in these circumstances. Oliver LJ stated what has to be proved to establish liability under this section, namely:

> First of all that the damage is of a kind which the animal, unless restricted, is likely to cause, or which, if caused, is likely to be severe; secondly - and I am paraphrasing now - the likelihood is due to characteristics of that animal that are not normally found in animals of that species, or which are not normally to be found except at particular times or at particular places: thirdly that these characteristics are also known to the keeper.

This does not quite accord with Lloyd LJ's view, but the important point in Oliver LJ's judgment was that the keeper must know the characteristics of the particular animal in these particular circumstances, and the rider in this case was not aware of the particular characteristic.

In order for there to be a successful claim under the Animals Act section 2 it must be proved that the injury or damage which has resulted from the incident is the sort of injury or damage which the animal is likely to cause in these circumstances and that the damage is likely to be serious. In addition the likelihood of the damage being serious must be due to the nature of the particular horse, which is not the normal nature of horses in the particular circumstances. The nature of the horse must be known to the keeper.

Curtis v Betts [1990]) gives further guidance in respect of s.2(2) of the Animals Act. This case involved a dog which bit a child. It was found that in order to satisfy s.2(2)(a) it must be shown that the damage caused was a kind which the particular animal was likely to cause unless restrained or which, if caused by that animal, was likely to be severe. It was not necessary to show that the animal had abnormal characteristics which made likely that if the animal caused damage, the damage would be severe.

For the purpose of s.2(2)(b) these must be a causal link between the characteristics of the animal and the damage suffered, and s.2(2)(b) should be read as if it referred simply to 'the damage' rather than to 'the likelihood of the damage or of its being severe'.

35

Knowledge

Knowledge must also be proved by the claimant and knowledge is not defined in the Act. The knowledge required must be the actual knowledge of the owner or person in possession, or constructive knowledge by reason of the actual knowledge of a servant or agent, who is in charge of the horse. The servant must actually be in charge of the horse and, where another servant is aware of the horse's propensities, this does not impute knowledge to the owner, if this servant is not in charge of the horse (*Maclean v The Forestry Commission* (1970)).

Knowledge can be proved by showing that the horse had a propensity to this type of behaviour and the best evidence is of previous similar behaviour or attempted previous behaviour. The knowledge must be of the precise characteristic displayed. In *Glanville v Sutton* [1928] a horse had been left tethered and muzzled in Ludgate Hill, and it attempted to bite the claimant, causing him injury. The defendants knew that the horse had a propensity to bite other horses, which was the reason for the muzzle. It was held that knowledge of an animal being dangerous in one respect, does not render a keeper liable if the animal proves to be dangerous in another respect.

It may be difficult to prove knowledge where the keeper of the animal is under sixteen. It cannot be taken for granted that every child under sixteen who is the keeper of a horse will tell their parents of the horse's unfortunate propensities.

Damage

Damage is defined in s.11 of the Animals Act 1971 as 'including the death of, or injury to, any person (including any disease and any impairment of physical or mental condition)'. It is clear that this definition is not intended to be exhaustive and, therefore, damage can mean any damage to property of another person, including animals. The horse's behaviour must have caused the damage suffered by the claimant. Unlike liability for negligence, where the test for remoteness is reasonable foresight, the test under this Act is directness of consequence. The two alternatives of damage in s.2(2)(a) do not in any way restrict the damage that can be subject to liability, and damage does not have to be severe to give the claimant a cause of action. The damage, however, must fall within s.2(1).

Straying

Section 4(1) of the Animals Act 1971 covers straying and provides '...where livestock belonging to another person strays on to land in the ownership or occupation of another, and
a) damage is done by the livestock to the land or to any property on it which is in the ownership or possession of another person; or
b) any expenses are reasonably incurred by that person in keeping the livestock while it cannot be restored to the person to whom it belongs or while it is detained in pursuance to section 7 of this Act or in ascertaining to whom it belongs;
the person to whom the livestock belong is liable for the damage or expenses except as otherwise provided for by this Act'.

Livestock is also defined in s.11 of the Act and includes horses. Before any action can be brought under this section, the claimant must be able to prove actual damage to his property, or that he has incurred reasonable expenses in keeping the horse until it is returned to its owner.

Anyone who has possession of the land, including a person who has grazing rights, can bring an action in trespass for straying animals. The person who is in possession and control of a horse is the person who is liable under this section. It follows therefore that, where a horse is with a trainer, the trainer rather than the owner would be responsible; similarly in a livery yard. Normally, however, it would be the owner who was responsible.

There are only two exceptions to liability under s.4 and these are again contained in s.5. These exceptions are:
(i) where the claimant is at fault; and
(ii) where livestock has strayed from the highway, when such livestock was present lawfully on the highway.

The latter exception really envisages cows being herded along the highway, although it might also cover the situation if a horse ridden on the road got loose and strayed off the highway.

Although s.5(1) provides the defence of fault of the claimant, where fencing is involved s.5(6) must be considered. This sub-section provides that:

'in determining whether any liability for damage under section 4 of this Act is excluded by sub-section (1) of this section, the damage shall not be treated as due to the fault of the person suffering it by reason only that he could have prevented it by fencing;

but a person is not liable under that section, where it is proved that the straying of livestock on the land would not have occurred, but for a breach by another person, being a person having an interest in the land, of a duty to fence.'

The combinations of subsections (1) and (6) mean that, where a horse strays because a fence has not been repaired and causes damage on another's land, if the landowner has a duty to maintain the fence, he cannot claim damages. Where there is no duty to maintain the fence, then the landowner can claim damages. He is even able to claim if he knew that the fence was defective and could have repaired it. Where the land has been leased to a third party and, as a result of straying, damage is caused to the third party's animals, the third party's right to sue will depend on whether or not the landowner had a duty to repair the fence. If he does, then the lessee can sue, if not, then he cannot.

Fencing is defined in s.11 of the Act, as 'the construction of any obstacle designed to prevent animals from straying'. The Act gives no such assistance on 'duty to fence'. Under the common law there has never been any legal obligation for a person to fence their land, but an obligation can arise through agreement; or through long use, or custom. Thus, where a person has always repaired his fences over many years, the law will assume that he thought he had a duty to do so and it would not be open, in those circumstances, to the person to say he had no duty. The person, himself, has created a liability which will also bind his successors in title.

The lawful presence on the highway means the right to pass and re-pass along the highway as already stated, and really envisages cows being herded along the road and trespassing into someone's garden. However, lawful presence is only a defence to the strict liability under the Act, and it may be open to a claimant to bring an action in negligence, provided there is evidence of negligence by the defendant.

Horses, or indeed animals in general, cannot be relied upon only to stray into neighbouring fields or from the highway onto other person's land, and s.8 of the Act covers the straying of animals onto the highway. Section 8(1) abolishes any common law rules which would exclude or restrict a person's liability in negligence for animals straying onto the highway. The ordinary principles of negligence apply (see Chapter 2).

There are, however, exceptions which are set out in s.8(2) of the Act, which cover 'Straying on to the highway'. The owner of straying animals will not be liable:

a) if the land is common land, and is land situated in an area where fencing is not customary, or it is a town or village green, and
b) the person placing the animal there had the right to place the animal on that land.

Remedies

A person whose land or property is damaged by a straying animal can make a claim for damages. He is also entitled, under s.7 of the Act, to detain the stray, provided that, at the time of straying, the animal is not under anyone's control. Having lawfully detained the animal, he has the right to sell it after fourteen days at a market or public auction. Both remedies, however, are not available; it must be one or the other. Whilst the animal is detained, it must be cared for, fed, and watered, and there is a duty to inform the police of the action within forty-eight hours. The police must then inform the owner if he is known. Where the animal is sold, the detainer is only entitled to keep such proceeds as cover the cost he has incurred, provided that the damage was caused by this particular incident of straying. The detainer is not entitled to keep any proceeds to cover damage caused by an earlier trespass.

Chapter 4 BUYING AND SELLING

Horses are treated as goods and chattels and, therefore, the law of buying and selling applies to them in the same way as buying and selling any other goods. The law which applies is a combination of case law and statute.

The purchase of a horse is an area full of potential difficulties as, in effect, the buyer is purchasing an unknown quantity, and it is difficult, if not impossible, to guard against latent defects.

The measure of protection for the buyer depends upon whether the sale is a private or business sale.

A private sale is one between two private individuals.

A business sale is where the seller carries on a business of buying and selling horses.

Whether a person is a horse dealer and, therefore, conducting a business sale is a question of fact, but even limited selling may be considered dealing and, therefore, a business.

The Sale of Goods Act 1979

The Sale of Goods Act 1979, apart from certain exceptions, repealed the Sale of Goods Act 1893 and now covers all contracts for the sale of goods made on or after 1 January 1894, whether in the course of business or not. The Act has been amended from time to time, most recently by the Sale and Supply of Goods Act 1994, which changed the use of the word 'condition' to 'term'. Somewhat confusingly at first sight, the terms referred to in the 1979 Act are still conditions of the contract (section 14(6) Sale of Goods Act 1979).

Under the Act as amended there are certain implied terms that a buyer can rely upon, although some of these will not apply to a private sale. These terms are:

1. That the vendor has the right to sell the horse (s.12(1)).
2. That the horse is reasonably fit for any purpose of which the seller has been informed (s.14(3)). The buyer, in those circumstances, is relying on the seller's skill or judgement. This applies whether or not the horse would normally be used for this purpose. There will not be an implied term if the buyer does not rely upon the skill or judgement of the seller or if it would be unreasonable for him to so rely. [It would not be prudent to rely upon the judgement of a seller who had no knowledge of the particular use for which the horse was required and, if the buyer did, then he could not rely upon this section if the sale went wrong.]
3. That the horse is not subject to any other interest of which the buyer has not been informed (s.12(2)).
4. That the horse is of satisfactory quality (s.14(2)). Satisfactory quality is defined in section 14(2A) and in the context of the sale of a horse it means that the horse must meet the standard that a reasonable person would regard as satisfactory taking account of the description of the horse, the price (if relevant) and all other relevant circumstances.

In considering the quality of goods under this section the court will take into account the state and condition of the horse or other goods and under s.14(2B) the following factors will be considered:

41

a) fitness for all purposes for which the goods in question are commonly supplied;

b) appearance and finish;

c) freedom from minor defects;

d) safety and

e) durability.

(This is not, however, an exclusive list; there may be other factors that the court will consider.)

As can be seen from the list, not all of these factors will apply to horses, but they are likely to apply to most equestrian equipment. There is no implied term in respect of defects drawn specifically to the buyer's attention before the contract is made. Where a buyer examines the horse before the contract is made, there is no such term in respect of defects which an examination ought to have revealed (s.14(2C)).

There is an implied term in all contracts for sale by description that the goods will correspond to the description (s.13(1)). It has been held that every item in a description which constitutes a substantial ingredient in the identity of the thing sold is a term (*Couchman v Hill* [1947]) and, where a horse bought in this way does not match the description, the buyer is entitled to return the horse or treat the breach as a breach of warranty and sue for damages.

In a private sale, there is no implied term or conditional warranty as to the merchantable quality of the horse or fitness for purpose of a horse, and the rule *caveat emptor* (buyer beware) applies.

Exclusion Clauses

A seller may seek to exclude certain liabilities by means of exclusion clauses. This area of the law is, largely, governed by the Unfair Contract Terms Act 1977. This Act provides some measure of protection for the buyer both in a consumer sale and a private one, although the protection is not the same.

In a consumer sale, liability for any breach of contract arising out of the implied terms already referred to, cannot be excluded or restricted by any term in the contract (Unfair Contract Terms Act 1977 s.7(1),(2)).

Section 11(1) of the 1977 Act provides that, where the sale is a private one (and a sale between two dealers is classed as a private sale), liability for breach of implied terms can be excluded or restricted by a term of the contract, providing such term were reasonable in all the circumstances, which were, or ought reasonably to have been known, or were in the contemplation of the parties when the contract was made.

In certain circumstances, the court may have to go further in considering the question of whether the term was reasonable. The factors that the court must take into account include:

(i) the strength of the relevant bargaining positions of the parties (Unfair Contract Terms Act 1977, s.6(3));

(ii) whether the buyer knew or ought to have known of the term (Unfair Contract Terms Act 1977, s.7(3)); and

(iii) whether the buyer received any inducement to agree to the term in question (Unfair Contract Terms Act 1977, s.7(4)).

Warranties and Conditions

There is a distinction in law between the more important and less important terms of a contract; these terms are known respectively as conditions and warranties (Unfair Contract Terms Act 1977, Sch.3).

There is some statutory assistance with conditions and warranties:

a) For the purposes of the Sale of Goods Act 1979, a warranty is defined in s.61(1) as an agreement, with reference to goods, which are the subject of a contract of sale, but collateral to the main purpose of such a contract, the breach of which gives rise to a claim for damages, but not the right to reject the goods and to treat the contract as repudiated.

b) The Sale of Goods Act 1979, s.11, also makes provision for conditions being construed as warranties, and the Act also provides that whether a particular term is a condition or warranty depends upon the construction of the contract.

In essence a warranty is a particular feature of the horse, for example that it is good to box, clip, catch or shoe. A condition is more fundamental to the contract, for example, that the animal has a proven track record.

On occasion the distinction between the two is difficult to discern and the terms have given rise to considerable case law. The matter is made more complicated by, for example, the fact that, in some circumstances, a warranty can amount to a condition.

The distinction is nevertheless important because the remedies available for breaches differ depending on how a term is construed. Where there is a breach of warranty, the buyer is entitled to damages (i.e. monetary compensation), but where there is a breach of condition then the buyer is entitled to repudiate the contract (i.e. return the horse).

When a horse being sold is described, the description can form part of the contract of sale.

A horse may be warranted as possessing certain attributes, or it may be a condition of the sale that the horse conforms to the description given. There is no particular form of words that is necessary to express a warranty. A warranty, in law, is really a statement of fact made before or during the sale transaction, before it is completed, provided that the statement is intended to be a warranty.

Whether the term is a condition or a warranty may depend on how that term is expressed by the parties at the time of sale. Where the seller of a horse says that the horse is sound, generally speaking, that would constitute a warranty. If, however, the vendor undertakes that he will take the horse back if it is not sound, then it is likely that the statement will have become a condition.

It would seem, therefore, that it is prudent for a buyer to obtain a warranty as to any qualities which he may require. It is also open to the buyer to insist that, if the horse does not possess the particular quality, then he will return it. In such circumstances, it will usually become a condition of the contract that the horse possesses such a quality.

A buyer should consider carefully what terms he wishes to include in the contract and whether they should be warranties or conditions. These then become the terms of the contract of sale.

Oral and written contracts

Whilst an oral contract has the same effect in law as a written contract, it would be advisable to have a written contract of sale setting out the terms of the agreement between the parties, including any terms which have been agreed as to the horse's qualities. Both parties should keep a copy of the contract so that, should a dispute arise, there is evidence of what the parties agreed. This is particularly important because, should a dispute come to court, it will be a question of fact for the court to decide whether the terms in question were warranties or conditions. The court, in deciding, will look to the intention of the parties at the time of the transaction and a written contract will provide good evidence.

Scope of warranties

What do warranties cover? First, it should be stated that they do not cover defects which are obvious. In an extreme example, it has been held that, if the seller guarantees that a horse has two eyes, he will not be liable if it has not, because the buyer could have examined the horse before he bought it (*Baily v Merrell* (1616)).

However, it may be that, on occasions, a buyer will not be present when the agreement to sell is made. In such a situation, the warranty will cover patent defects. Similarly, where a seller, in order to prevent a buyer from examining a horse and discovering an obvious defect, warrants the horse, or if a seller tries to conceal an obvious defect, then the horse will be covered by the warranty.

When a horse is given a warranty on sale, that horse should possess the qualities referred to in the warranty and where it is warranted to be free from vice or a particular vice, the horse should be free from such vice(s). A seller should limit any warranty to cover matters of which he is aware, because a general warranty does not allow the seller to claim that he did not know of the particular vice.

A declaration that the buyer can depend upon the horse being 'perfectly quiet and free from vice' is a warranty even though the actual word is not used. Where the word 'warrant' is used, the warranty will only cover any descriptions that it refers to specifically. Hence, where a horse was described as 'a black gelding, five years old, quiet to ride and drive, warranted sound', the only warranty was as to the horse's soundness. The horse was not warranted to be quiet to ride and drive. Sometimes, the word 'warranted' may be used alone in describing a horse. In these circumstances, it refers only to the animal's soundness and to no other preceding description. A seller can limit any warranty but, where a horse is described and warranted as sound and quiet in all respects, that is exactly what it means and includes being ridden, being in harness, in the stable or in the field.

Generally, when horses are sold, they are warranted in respect of soundness and lack of vices, but that does not limit any warranties the seller may wish to make; anything relevant may be included.

Warranties do, however, only cover the facts as they are at the time of sale, unless expressly covering a future event. It is a question of fact, whether a defect is a patent (i.e. obvious) one or is latent, and whether the buyer used ordinary care in any examination of the horse he undertook. In addition, a court will have to decide as a matter of fact whether any statement made was intended to be a warranty and part of the contract of sale.

Unsoundness

Unsoundness is likely to cause the most difficulties when buying or selling a horse and it has produced considerable case law. Unsoundness was defined by Baron Parke in *Coates v Stephens* (1838) in this way:

> If at the time of sale a horse has any disease or defect which actually diminishes, or in its ordinary progress will diminish, its normal usefulness, it is not sound.

It was held in that case that a cough was an unsoundness and Baron Parke further made it quite clear that the condition must exist at the time of sale. Baron Parke confirmed this decision in *Kiddell v Burnard* (1842), adding that unsoundness was anything which diminished the ordinary usefulness of the horse.

A congenital defect, present from birth, which at the time of sale renders the horse less than fit for reasonable use is unsoundness (*Holliday v Morgan* (1858)). In this particular case, the defect was a convexity of the eye making the horse short-sighted so that it was liable to shy.

Even a temporary lameness existing at the time of sale, which renders the horse unfit for present use, is breach of warranty of soundness. It is not necessary that any disorder should be permanent or incurable, only that it is present at the time of sale (*Elfan v Brogden* (1815)).

These cases are nineteenth-century cases, most of which were tried by a judge and jury. A jury was a particularly suitable tribunal for deciding soundness because it is a question of fact. Nowadays, cases of this nature are tried by a judge only, but the question whether or not a horse is unsound is still one of fact (*Lewis v Peake* (1861)).

Vices

A vice is not necessarily the same as unsoundness. Vice has been defined as 'a defect in the temper of the horse which makes it dangerous or diminishes its usefulness, or a bad habit which is injurious to its health' (*Scholefield v Robb* (1839)). Crib-biting has been held to be a vice; if the crib-biting could be shown to be injurious to the horse's health it could be argued that it was an unsoundness. As a general principle, unsoundness relates to physical defects, while vices are concerned with the horse's temperament.

It should be noted that most of the case law is nineteenth-century and there have been considerable advances in veterinary science. It may be that what were considered unsoundness and vice would be different in the light of such advances. Equally, it could be argued that conditions of health or temperament that were not considered vices or unsoundness may be considered so now in the light of veterinary advances. The law is ever-moving!

Giving of warranties by agents

If a person is given the authority to sell a horse and, therefore, is acting as an agent, it does not necessarily mean that the person has the authority to give a warranty. However, if a groom were asked to conduct a sale for an owner it would take very little evidence to show that the groom had the authority to warrant the animal he was selling.

There is a distinction to be made between the assistant or groom of a private seller and a horse dealer's assistant. If, when purchasing a horse from a dealer, the transaction is conducted with a servant or assistant, then the buyer is entitled to assume that the servant has the authority to warrant the horse. Therefore, where a horse dealer's assistant gives a warranty, even if he has been expressly forbidden to do so, it will still bind the dealer. Where a groom with no authority from the owner warrants a horse, the owner is not bound by the warranty (*Brady v Todd* (1861)). An exception, however, would be where the sale took place at a horse fair or auction (*Brooks v Hassell* (1883)).

Where a servant is employed to sell a horse and receive the price he has an implied authority to warrant the horse (*Alexander v Gibson* (1811)).

Anything said on delivery of the horse cannot usually amount to a warranty.

Breaches of warranties

What happens if there is a breach? In simple terms, as stated earlier, if there is a breach of warranty, the buyer is entitled to claim for damages for that breach. However, if it is a breach of condition, the buyer can return the horse. The level of damages is likely to be the difference between the amount paid for the horse and the value of the horse without the matter subject of the warranty.

If a complaint is to be made, it is usually important that the seller is informed as soon as possible of any likely breach, either of a warranty or a condition. Provided that there is no time limit imposed by the original contract, within which any complaint must be made, in general terms, the buyer will not be prejudiced by anything he has done before he discovered the defect.

Subject to certain exceptions (e.g. deceit, fraud or an unreasonably short time limit), where a purchaser has reserved the right to return the horse within a specified time, then the horse must be returned before the expiration of that limit. However, a buyer does not have to return the horse as soon as he discovers the defect, if it is before the specified time expires. If, therefore, the horse is discovered to be injured, through no fault of the buyer, then, after the defect is discovered, but within the time limit, the buyer is not liable and can still return the horse.

If the circumstances are such that the horse is so badly injured that it cannot be returned at all within the time limit, then the fact that it has not been returned by the buyer within the time limit will not usually prevent the buyer from bringing an action for breach of warranty, provided the seller is informed within the time limit (*Chapman v Withers* (1888)).

If, unfortunately, the animal dies, within the specified time, then the loss will fall on the seller, provided that the buyer is not at fault.

It should also be borne in mind that, where a seller warrants a horse and the buyer then resells the horse with some warranty of which there is a breach, then the first buyer is entitled to join the seller as a third party. If the seller does not involve himself in the action, the first buyer is entitled to his costs and any damages as agent for the seller (*Lewis v Peake* (1861)).

Trial before purchase

It is not unusual for a horse to be taken on trial before purchase, and both parties to this type of arrangement should exercise caution. It would be prudent to set out in writing the terms of any such arrangements, because, although normally the transaction goes through without any problems, if problems do arise, with nothing in writing, it may be difficult for either party to support a justifiable claim.

Any agreement should state clearly:
a) that it is a loan agreement
b) the duration of the loan
c) the purpose of the loan, i.e. trial with a view to purchase
d) transport arrangements
e) insurance arrangements
f) the fact that the horse remains in the ownership of the seller at all times
g) any other specific conditions that the seller wishes to make.

Minors

A large number of horses, and more particularly ponies, are or may be owned by minors (i.e. a person under the age of eighteen years).

49

It is therefore necessary to be extremely careful where a minor is involved in either the buying or selling of a horse. Generally speaking, minors do not have the legal capacity to enter into a contract, and, therefore, cannot be sued on some contracts. Section 3(1) of the Minors' Contracts Act 1987 provides some relief for a claimant suing a defendant who is a minor, in that where a minor has acquired property as a result of entering into a contract which is unenforceable against him, he may be ordered to transfer that property back to the claimant. If a child is involved in either buying or selling a horse, it is prudent to make enquiry and any contract, to be valid, should be made with an adult. In addition, a buyer should not rely on any warranty in respect of a horse or pony made by a minor.

Auctions

Auctions have given rise to a significant amount of case law. An auctioneer is a person who carries on a business requiring skill and knowledge and must, therefore, display such skill and knowledge when acting for a vendor, as is reasonably expected from competent auctioneers. Actions can arise in negligence (see Chapter 2) as well as in contract. There are three main contractual relationships:
1. Between the buyer and the auctioneer.
2. Between the seller and the auctioneer.
3. Between the buyer and the seller.

It is important to appreciate that the auctioneer's request for bids is simply that, and the bid constitutes the offer, which it is open to the auctioneer to accept or reject. The contract between the buyer and the auctioneer occurs once the bid has been accepted and the hammer falls.

Auctions of horses are, therefore, another area where the buyer should be cautious. The buyer should always examine a horse before bidding for it, because, as a general rule, an auctioneer cannot himself give a warranty on a horse unless he has express instructions from the seller. An auctioneer has no implied authority to warrant (*Payne v Lord Beaconsfield* (1882)) and an unauthorised warranty by an auctioneer will not bind the seller.

As always, the general rule is subject to certain qualifications. Where statements of fact are printed in an auctioneer's catalogue, which confer an additional value on the horse sold, these can amount to warranties. Where the auctioneer's catalogue of horses to be sold by auction added the words 'in foal to Warlock' after the description of a mare and other mares were described as 'having been served by' it was held that, looking at the descriptions used in respect of other mares and the nature of the facts represented, the words in question must be taken to have been intended by the parties to be a warranty (*Gee v Lucas* (1867)). The principle is subject to the qualification that the fact stated must be one which might be within the party's knowledge, or that he might have the means or possibility of knowing (*Gee v Lucas* (1867)).

When buying at auction it is always advisable to read the conditions of sale carefully. If, however, the seller makes an oral statement at the sale, even though such statement would, in the normal course of events, only amount to a warranty, it can still override the conditions of sale. In *Couchman v Hill* [1947] a heifer was described in the auction catalogue as 'a red and white heifer unserved'. The catalogue stated that 'all lots must be taken subject to all faults or errors of description (if any) and no compensation will be paid for the same'. The conditions of sale stated that the lots were sold with all faults, and errors of description, and that the auctioneers were not responsible for the correct description, genuineness or authenticity of, or any fault or defect in any lot, and they gave no warranty whatsoever. Before the actual sale of the heifer, whilst it was in the ring, the defendant (seller) was asked by the claimant (buyer) and the auctioneer to confirm that the heifer was unserved, which the defendant did. Some time after the purchase, the heifer suffered a miscarriage and later died from the strain of carrying a calf too young. The claimant claimed damages for breach of warranty, and it was held, *inter alia*, that the description 'unserved' constituted a condition, on the basis that every item in a description, which constitutes a substantial ingredient in the identity of the thing sold, is a condition. It was, however, open to the claimant to waive the condition and treat the description as a warranty and claim for damages. It was also

51

held that the conversation between the parties before the sale amounted to a warranty which overrode the condition in the printed terms and the contract was made on the basis that the animal was 'warranted' not to have been served.

An earlier case, *Hopkins v Tanqueray* (1854), which came to a different decision, was not cited in *Couchman v Hill* and it was thought that, had the case been cited, the court might have come to a different conclusion. *Hopkins v Tanqueray* was, however, cited in *Harling v Eddy* [1951], which involved similar facts to *Couchman v Hill*. It was distinguished, on the basis that the conversation, which could have amounted to a warranty, had been held on the day prior to the sale.

Mistake

It is not unknown for one or both parties to a contract to be mistaken as to some area of the contract. If there is a mistake the remedy can either be in common law or in equity.

At common law there are four bases of relief:

1. In actions to recover money paid under a mistake of fact.
2. In actions to recover property which was prevented from passing by reason of mistake.
3. In actions to recover damages in respect of mistake induced by fraudulent or non-fraudulent misrepresentation.
4. As a defence in actions of contract, where a mistake of fact was of such a nature as to prevent the formation of a contract in law.

In equity there is a further area which could affect a horse owner, namely proceedings could be taken to recover money paid or other assets transferred by mistake.

Although mistakes may arise for many reasons, for example ignorance, forgetfulness or misconception, the law itself makes little distinction. Mistakes are either:

a) such that prevent there being real consent to a transaction or
b) such that mean that there is a complete failure to express properly in writing the intention of the parties to the purported agreement.

Mistakes may be of law or of fact. A mistake of fact is likely to be either:

1. A mistake as to the nature of the transaction.
2. A mistake as to who the other party to the transaction is.
3. A mistake as to the subject matter, whether it be identity or some material fact about the subject matter or the terms of the transaction.

Where a buyer believes he is buying a horse from a particular person, perhaps someone well known in the horse world, but in fact is mistaken, there would be no contract. Where, however, a buyer thought he was buying from A, but was in fact buying from B, and it did not matter to the buyer then, provided there was no fraud, the contract would be valid.

Where a mistake occurs as to the identity of a horse being sold then there is no contract. If, however, there is evidence to show that the parties, despite the mistake, still intended to contract in respect of that particular horse, then there is a contract (see *Raffles v Wichelhaus* (1864)).

Where there is a mistake of fact which is material to the subject matter of the contract, then the contract is likely to be void *ab initio* (i.e. it never existed). This could arise where a buyer was contracting to buy a mare in foal to a particular sire, but the mare was not in foal at all.

Where a person seeks relief on the grounds of mistake, he must prove that he acted as he did because of the mistake. If he would have acted the same, even if he had not made the mistake, then he is not entitled to any relief. The mistake must be fundamental to the transaction.

Relief will be granted if the mistake was due to ignorance, even if the party alleging the mistake had the means of knowing the true facts. Where the mistake was due to misconception, and possibly forgetfulness, the court will also grant relief. Such relief is likely to be recovery of money paid or recovery of the horse, rescission of the contract or damages for breach of contract.

Misrepresentation

A representation is a statement made by person as to a matter of fact. It can be an oral or a written statement or can arise by implication from words or conduct. The matter of fact can relate to a present or past fact. A representation is not a contractual term.

Where a person makes a false representation which results in another person entering into a contract with him, then the person to whom the false representation was made can elect to rescind (or end) the contract.

The person who seeks to end the contract may ask the court to declare his right to end the contract and the court may then order the return of money paid or chattels handed over in pursuance of the contract. He will also be able to use the fact of ending the contract due to the false misrepresentations as a defence in an action for enforcement of the contract.

At common law, the remedy will not include damages for any loss suffered as a result of the misrepresentation unless it can be shown that the false representation was made fraudulently or negligently. Under the Misrepresentation Act 1967 s.2(1), if a person enters into a contract after a misrepresentation has been made and suffers a loss as a result, he may be awarded damages despite the absence of fraud, unless the person making the representation can prove that he had reasonable grounds to believe it was true and did so up to the time the contract was made.

Generally, damages for injury as a result of misrepresentation are not recoverable unless it can be shown that:
a) the representation was false and fraudulent
b) it was negligent
c) it was made by another party to the contract who is unable to show that he believed that representation to be true.

Failing to disclose information can amount to a misrepresentation. In other words, the misrepresentation can be due to omitting to mention some relevant matter as well as incorrectly stating some fact.

If a horse is purchased and there is a misrepresentation, then the buyer will be entitled to rescind the contract (i.e. to send the horse back). In certain circumstances, he may be entitled to damages for any loss suffered.

If there is negligence or fraud in the representation then the horse can be sent back and a claim for damages for any loss made. In *Naughton v O'Callaghan* (*Independent* 22 February 1990), it was held that the measure of damages for negligent misrepresentation in respect of the horse's pedigree was the difference between its purchase price and it fallen value after a poor performance on the race track. Further, it was held that, in this particular case, it would have been unjust to take the damages as the difference between the purchase price and its actual value at the time of the acquisition.

Veterinary Certificates

Unless the seller is prepared to make statements as to the horse's qualities, the buyer is in a very precarious position. Where the seller is a dealer, there are certain safeguards, i.e. the implied conditions under the Sale of Goods Act, but in a private sale there is little help for the buyer. It is advisable, when purchasing any horse (but essential when purchasing a horse where nothing is said), to call in a veterinary surgeon to examine the horse and give a certificate. A veterinary certificate is a limited form of guarantee in respect of the purchase and is well worth the cost. A veterinary surgeon giving such a certificate is exercising his professional skill in examining the horse. When doing so, he must exercise the ordinary skill which is to be expected of a member of the veterinary profession. He is expected to spot any defect which a prudent and careful veterinary surgeon would have spotted. If he fails to do so or makes a mistake, he could be liable to a claim in negligence provided that the purchaser relied upon the veterinary surgeon's opinion.

Veterinary surgeons are, of course, aware of their duties and the pitfalls. They are therefore reluctant to give any warranty that a horse is sound. The definition of soundness and the case law on what constitutes soundness have contributed to this reluctance. A veterinary test on a prospective purchase involves stages and, if the horse passes, the vet is likely to certify that he can find no reason why the horse should not be used for the purpose for which it is required.

A seller may obtain his own veterinary certificate for the horse and offer it with the animal. The difficulty here is that the veterinary surgeon is effectively acting for both parties. Nevertheless, in certain circumstances, even though the buyer has no contractual relationship with the veterinary surgeon, he may be entitled to sue him if he was negligent. The veterinary surgeon, however, would have to have been aware, at the time of making the examination, that the certificate was to be used as a guarantee of the horse's soundness and that a buyer might decide to buy the horse on the strength of that certificate.

Trade Descriptions Acts

The Trade Descriptions Acts 1968 and 1972 are Acts intended to protect the customer. They apply only to persons carrying on a business and, for an offence to be committed, the transaction must be an integral part of the business (*Davies v Sumner* [1984] 3 All ER 831 and *Devlin v Hall* (1990) Crim LR 879).

The 1968 Act prohibits false trade descriptions and creates certain powers as to the definition of terms, marking of goods and display of information in advertisements (ss.1–10). The Act also sets out offences, makes provision for certain defences, and gives powers of enfranchisement (ss.18–31).

The 1972 Act deals with imported goods and provides for indication of their origin, relevant to saddlery and equipment.

Any person who, in the course of a trade or business, applies a false trade description to any goods, or supplies or offers to supply any goods to which a false trade description is applied, commits an offence (Trade Description Act 1968, s.1). These Acts will apply to horse dealers and to the sellers of saddlery and other equestrian equipment.

Chapter 5 PROTECTION FROM CRUELTY

It is hoped that responsible horse owners would not be cruel to their equine friends. However, this chapter is included to clarify what constitutes cruelty and to identify the penalties that are laid down for it by statute. It must be incumbent upon all responsible horse owners to look out for and try to prevent cruelty to horses, whether caused by ignorance or a deliberate act.

Protection of Animals Acts and Associated Legislation

The main statute governing this area of the law is the Protection of Animals Act 1911. This Act, which has been amended by several further Acts over the years up to 1964, consolidated the legislation already in force. These Acts are general cited as the Protection of Animals Acts 1911 to 1964, although a further Act, the Protection of Animals (Penalties) Act 1987, was passed to increase the penalties for cruelty to animals.

In addition, two further acts have been passed. The Protection Against Cruel Tethering Act 1988 amended the Protection of Animals Act 1911, adding Section 1(1)(f). This protects horses, asses and mules against tethering carried out in a manner which is likely to cause unnecessary suffering, which is now an offence under the Act.

The Protection of Animals (Amendment) Act 1988 enables the court to disqualify a person from having custody of an animal on a first conviction for cruelty. Under this Act, penalties for offences relating to animal fights are increased, and further provision is made in respect of attendance of such fights in England and Wales and attendance in Scotland is also penalised under the Act.

The above-mentioned Acts provide that a number of offences against animals shall be offences of cruelty. A conviction for such an offence renders the offender liable to a fine or imprisonment not exceeding six months, or both.

Under the Protection of Animals Act 1911, s.2. the Magistrates' Court also has the power to make orders of compensation, deprivation of ownership or destruction of the animal (see also the Protection of Animals (Amendment) Act 1988). There is also the power to disqualify a person from keeping a riding establishment. A second conviction gives the court the power to disqualify a person from having custody of any animal.

With one exception set out in the Protection of Animals Act 1911, s.1(1)(d), the prosecution will not have to prove that an act was done wilfully or intentionally: all it will have to prove is that pain and suffering were caused and that the pain and suffering constitute cruelty. Where, however, the charge is one of causing or procuring a cruel act, then the prosecution do have to prove guilty knowledge, and where an offender's guilty knowledge has to be proved, it is not enough to show that, if the offender had done his job properly, he would have known of the suffering. The offender must have actually known of the suffering (*Elliot v Osborn* [1891]).

Defining cruelty

Cruelty has to be defined, and what may not have been considered cruel by earlier authorities may well be considered cruel now.

Simply to inflict pain on an animal is not necessarily cruelty. No one could argue, for instance that castrating a horse was not inflicting pain, but this is not cruelty under the Acts. In the case of *Budge v Parsons* (1863), Wightman J said that cruelty is 'the unnecessary abuse of the animal'. Further definitions have included 'the wilful causing of pain to an animal without justification for so doing' and 'causing unnecessary suffering' (*Barnard v Evans* [1925]).

Section 1(1)(a) of the Protection of Animals Act 1911 sets out the offences of cruelty, namely, if any person:

a) shall cruelly beat, kick, ill-treat, override, over-drive, over-load, torture, infuriate, or terrify any animal, or shall cause or procure, or being the owner, permit any animal to be so used, or shall, by wantonly or unreasonably doing or omitting to do any act, or causing or procuring the commission or omission of any act, cause any unnecessary suffering, or, being the owner, permit any unnecessary suffering to be so caused to any animal; or

b) shall convey or carry, or cause to procure, or being the owner, permit to be conveyed or carried, any animal in such manner or position as to cause that animal any unnecessary suffering; or

c) shall cause, procure, or assist at the fighting or baiting of any animal; or shall keep, use, manage, or act or assist in the management of, any premises or place for the purpose, or partly for the purpose of fighting or baiting any animal, or shall permit any premises or place to be so kept, managed, or used, or shall receive, or cause or procure any person to receive, money for the admission of any person to such premises or place; or

d) shall wilfully, without any reasonable cause or excuse, administer, or cause or procure, or being the owner permit, such administration of, any poisonous or injurious drug or substance to any animal, or shall wilfully, without any reasonable cause or excuse, cause any such substance to be taken by any animal; or

e) shall subject, or cause or procure, or being the owner permit to be subjected, any animal to any operation which is performed without due care and humanity;

f) shall tether any horse, ass or mule under such conditions as to cause the animal unnecessary suffering;

they are guilty of an offence of cruelty and will be liable to the penalties imposed under the Protection of Animals (Penalties) Act 1987.

The important word in section 1(1)(a) is cruelly. This is the offence. The words that follow are examples, and each one constitutes a single offence. Cruelty is not only doing a cruel act, but may also be a cruel omission.

Section 1(1)(b) covers the carriage of horses, and an owner of a horse that is transported in such a way as to cause unnecessary suffering will also be guilty.

Under section 7 of the 1911 Act, any person who impounds an animal must supply it with sufficient food or water; failure to do so can constitute an offence.

An owner of an animal can be deemed to have permitted cruelty if he failed to exercise reasonable care and supervision in respect of the protection of the animal from cruelty (Protection of Animals Act 1911, s.1(2)). Unusually, the onus of proving the care and supervision, on a balance of probabilities, rests on the owner. This may fall foul of the Human Rights Act 1999, which came into force on 2 October 2000. Article 6 of the European Convention on Human Rights states that a defendant is innocent until proven guilty. A defendant should not have to prove his innocence.

Exemptions

Section 1 of the Protection of Animals Act does not, however, make illegal lawful experiments on animals, carried out under the Animals (Scientific Procedures) Act 1986, nor does it apply to the destruction of animals for food, unless this caused unnecessary suffering. The coursing or hunting of any captive animal is also excluded unless the animal has been liberated in an injured, mutilated or exhausted condition.

Operations on animals

Operations on animals which are performed without due care and humanity are illegal and anyone who causes or procures such an operation, or as an owner permits it, is guilty of cruelty.

All operations on animals performed without anaesthetics to prevent pain are deemed to be carried out without due care and humanity, save certain exceptions which include:

(i) The making of injections or extractions by the use of a hollow needle.

(ii) The rendering in emergency of first aid.

(iii) Any procedure under the Animals (Scientific Procedures) Act 1986.

(iv) Any minor operation performed by a veterinary surgeon or veterinary practitioner which, because of its nature, is normally carried out without anaesthetic.

(v) Any minor operation which is not necessarily performed by a veterinary practitioner. (Although this is within the legislation it is not easy to envisage what it refers to.)

The exceptions may be changed by the Minister of Agriculture Fisheries and Food, The Secretary of State for Wales and the Secretary of State for Scotland acting jointly and after consultation with the Royal College of Veterinary Surgeons and any other relevant body.

Other Practices Subject to Legislation

Abandonment

Under the Abandonment of Animals Act 1960 s.1 it is an offence of cruelty for any person who is the owner, or is in charge or in control of any animal, to abandon the animal without reasonable cause or excuse in circumstances likely to cause the animal to suffer. Such abandonment may be temporary or permanent.

Docking and nicking

Although at one time a common practice, docking and nicking of horses was prohibited by the Docking and Nicking of Horses Act 1949, s 1. The exception to this is if a member of the Royal College of Veterinary Surgeons certifies in writing that this operation is necessary in his opinion for the horse's health because of an injury to or disease of the tail. Anyone acting in breach of this section is guilty of an offence which is triable summarily and subject upon conviction to a fine or imprisonment not exceeding three months, or both.

Humane slaughter

Under the Protection of Animals Act 1911, s.11 a police constable has the power to slaughter any animal that, in the opinion of a veterinary surgeon, is so severely diseased or injured that it is cruel to keep it alive. This may be particularly relevant where a horse has been injured as a result of a car accident, distressing though it may be for the horse owner.

Performing horses

It is within this legislation that performing horses are given some protection. Anyone exhibiting or training performing horses must be registered with the local authority in accordance with the Performing Animals (Regulations) Act 1925, s.1. This does not, however, include horses in training for genuine military, police, agricultural or sporting purposes. Under the Performing Animals (Regulations) Act 1925, s.4(2), a registered person, if convicted of an offence, either under that Act or the Protection of Animals Acts, may have his name removed from the register and may be disqualified, either permanently or for a period of time, from being registered. Where it has been proved in the Magistrates' Court that the training or exhibition of a performing animal has been accompanied by cruelty, and should be prohibited or allowed only subject to conditions, the court may also prohibit the training or exhibition of an animal, or allow it only upon certain conditions. There is a right of appeal and any order made does not come into force until the expiration of seven days from the making of the order or until any appeal has been heard (Performing Animals (Regulations) Act 1925, s.2(1)–(3)).

The Protection of Animals Act 1934, s.1, provides that persons promoting, permitting or taking part in public performances which include the throwing or casting, with ropes or other appliances, of any unbroken horse commit an offence. Equally, riding or attempting to ride any horse which has been stimulated to make it buck, by any appliance or treatment involving cruelty, is also guilty of an offence.

Under the Cinematograph Films (Animals) Act 1937, s.1, the film industry is not allowed to show a film for public exhibition if there are scenes in it which involved any cruel infliction of pain or terror on any animals. Nor is the goading of any animal to fury allowed.

Registration of farriers

The relevant legislation here is the Farrier's (Registration) Act 1975 as amended by the Farriers (Registration) (Amendment) Act 1977.

According to the preamble, these Acts were passed 'to prevent and avoid suffering by and cruelty to horses arising from the shoeing thereof by unskilled persons'. With the intention of promoting the proper shoeing of horses by ensuring that farriers are trained, this legislation established the Farrier's Registration Council to register farriers, and makes illegal the shoeing of horses by unqualified persons.

Under the Act, the general function of establishing and maintaining standards and conduct amongst farriers is given to the Worshipful Company of Farriers. Under section 2, The Act also establishes a Registration Council to compile and administer a register of persons engaged in shoeing, provided they are qualified and have applied for registration and paid the appropriate fee (s.3). The qualifications for registration are set out in section 7.

The Act also provides for certificates of registrates (s.10), approval of courses (s.11), supervision of approved institutions and examinations (s.12), investigation and disciplinary committees (ss.13 and 14) and the removal of names from the register (s.15).

Section 15A as inserted by the Farriers (Registration) (Amendment) Act 1977 provides that it is an offence for an unregistered person to use or adopt the style, title or description 'farrier' or 'shoeing smith' or any other style, title or description which is likely to cause any other person to believe that he is registered. This section does not apply to a person who has had his name removed from the register but has not yet been notified, nor to a person who has applied for registration but has not had the application determined. Anyone who contravenes this section shall be liable on summary conviction to a fine.

Section 16 is an important section in that it establishes certain offences namely:

(i) for an unregistered person to carry out any farriery

(ii) for a person registered in Part III of the register to carry out farriery by way of trade or for reward.

The exceptions to the above are:

(i) A person serving under articles of apprenticeship.

(ii) A person attending an approved training course at an approved institution.

(iii) A veterinary surgeon or a veterinary practitioner.

(iv) A person undergoing training as a veterinary surgeon who is supervised by a veterinary surgeon, veterinary practitioner or a person registered under the Act.

(v) A person rendering first aid in an emergency to a horse.

The offences are all summary offences and offenders are liable to a fine not exceeding level 3 on the standard scale.

A final offence is under section 5, which deals with fraudulent entries on the register. It is an offence 'wilfully to procure or attempt to procure the entry of a person's name in the register by making or producing or causing to be made or produced any false or fraudulent representation or declaration, either orally or in writing'. The penalty is again on summary conviction a fine not exceeding level three.

The Farrier's Registration Council keeps and maintains a register of farriers. In order to be included on the register the Council must be satisfied that the farrier has gained the adequate experience and expertise. It is within the Council's ambit to approve training courses and qualification, and it is under a duty to keep itself informed of the nature of instruction given at institutions approved by the Council, and of the examinations set.

There is an investigating committee which acts for the preliminary investigation of cases and to decide whether a disciplinary case ought to be referred to the disciplinary committee. The disciplinary committee is also set up by this Act for the consideration and determination of disciplinary cases. This committee deals with appeals against refusal of registration and failure to register the applicant in the appropriate part of the register. Most importantly, the disciplinary committee also deals with the removal or suspension of names from the register in instances where there has been serious professional misconduct, or where a person was not, in fact, qualified for registration at the time he registered, or if a person has been convicted of an offence of cruelty to animals.

If a person's name is removed from the register, that person must be notified and has twenty-eight days to appeal against this to the High Court or, in Scotland, the Court of Session. A decision of these courts is final.

Chapter 6 IMPORT, EXPORT AND MOVEMENT OF HORSES

The Animal Health Act 1981 provides the basis for legislation which covers the import, export and movement of horses. Under this Act the Minister of Agriculture (or his equivalent under the devolved assemblies in Scotland and Wales) has wide powers to prohibit and regulate the import of animals, including horses and ponies, whether by sea or air into Great Britain. In this context Great Britain includes England, Wales and Scotland, but excludes the Channel Islands and the Isle of Man.

Supplementary to the Animal Health Act are such orders as may be made by the Minister. The main order now governing the importing and exporting of animals is the Animal and Animal Products (Import and Export) Regulations 1998, which implement the European Community directives. It is prohibited to export, import or transport for intra community trade any animal to which one of the specific directives applies, except in compliance with that directive.

Prevention of Suffering in Transit

There are general provisions under the Animal Health Act 1981 to ensure the prevention of suffering (s.37) and the adequate provision of food and water (s.38) to animals, including horses, that are being transported. This is further emphasised by the Welfare of Animals (Transport) Order 1997 which provides for the welfare of animals, which include horses, when being transported. This order makes general provision for the protection of animals in transit, and additionally it makes provision for:

a) space allowance
b) fitness of animals to travel
c) treatment of sick animals
d) feeding and watering
e) travelling times and rest periods
f) accompaniment by competent persons
g) duties of transporters
h) transport of animals by air
i) route plans
j) animal transport certificates
k) exceptions
l) import and export to third countries
m) enforcement inspectors' powers
n) plans of the vessel
o) offences

The transport of animals by road and rail is covered by the Transit of Animals (Road and Rail) Order 1975 as amended in 1995 and 1997.

Transport by sea is covered by the Horses (Sea Transport) Order 1952 as amended in 1997 and applies to horses carried in vessels to or from a port in Great Britain. The provisions cover a variety of areas, but in particular there are provisions for stalls, space, drainage, overcrowding and fire-fighting. There are restrictions on carrying horses in open barges and requirements that, where a horse is insufficiently protected from the elements by its natural coat, it should wear a rug.

Import

The importation of animals from third countries (i.e. outside the European Union) is prohibited unless certain conditions are complied with, the import takes place at a specified border inspection post, and the specified procedure is followed. There is separate provision for the importation of animals from outside the Community where checks have been carried out in another member state.

Veterinary inspectors have powers which include entry inspection and examination.

Any breach of the statutory provisions is an offence punishable on summary conviction by a fine or up to three months imprisonment or, on conviction on indictment, by an unlimited fine or up to two years imprisonment, or both.

Under the Docking and Nicking of Horses Act 1949, docked horses from outside the United Kingdom (this includes the Channel Islands and the Isle of Man), cannot be landed unless permitted by Customs or licensed by the Minister (s.2(1)). Customs will not permit any entry unless the animal is to be re-exported as soon as possible. A licence will not be granted unless the Minister is satisfied that the equine will be used for breeding (s.2(3)). An illegal landing of a docked horse is an offence under s.2(3) of the Act, as is making a false statement in order to obtain permission of a licence under s.2(4).

Section 10 of the Animal Health Act 1981, which covers importation, allows the Minister to make such provisions as are necessary for the prevention or introduction or spread of disease. This issue is dealt with further under Diseases, later in this chapter.

Export

The exportation of animals is not prohibited by law. However, the Minister has certain powers under the Animal Health Act, which specifically covers the exporting of horses, which in this context includes asses, mules and ponies. Ponies are also subject to specific provisions relating to them alone (see below).

Section 40 of the Animal Health Act 1981 restricts the export of horses and mules and makes it an offence to ship or attempt to ship any horse (not including ponies) in any vessel or aircraft from any port or aerodrome inside Great Britain to any port or aerodrome outside the British Isles, unless the horse:

a) immediately before shipment has been examined by a veterinary inspector appointed by the Minister to examine under this section, and

b) has been certified in writing by the inspector to comply with the conditions set out in subsection (2).

The pertinent conditions are:

a) that the horse is capable of being conveyed to the port or aerodrome outside the British Islands and disembarked without cruelty, and

b) that the horse is capable of being worked without suffering.

Section 40(3) imposes further conditions, namely that, where the inspector is satisfied that the equine is either a heavy draught horse, a vanner, mule or jennet or an ass, then he must also be satisfied that it is less than eight years old and of a value not less than those set below:

A heavy duty horse	£715
A vanner, mule or jennet	£495
An ass	£220

Subsection (3) does not, however, apply in the case of any horse where the inspector is satisfied:

a) that it is intended to use the horse as a performing animal, or

b) that the horse is registered in the stud book of a society for the encouragement of horse-breeding recognised by the Minister and the horse is intended to be used for breeding or exhibition, or

c) that the horse is a foal at foot, accompanying a horse described in paragraph (b) above.

This is a rather dated provision, but remains on the statute book.

Specific provisions for ponies

Section 41 of the Animal Health Act 1981 covers the restrictions in respect of the export of ponies. Ponies are defined in s.89(1) as 'any horse measuring not more than 147 centimetres in height except a foal travelling with its dam if the dam exceeds that height'.

This section makes it an offence to export ponies unless:

a) the appropriate Minister is satisfied that the pony is intended for riding, breeding or exhibition, and

   (i)   its value exceeds £300, or

   (ii) in the case of a pony not exceeding 122 centimetres in height other than a Shetland pony, not exceeding 107 centimetres, its value exceeds £220, or

   (iii) in the case of a Shetland pony its value exceeds £145, or

   (iv) such other value in any of the cases as may be prescribed by order of the Ministers, and

b) that immediately before shipment the pony has been individually inspected by a veterinary inspector and has been certified in writing by the inspector to be capable of being taken to the port or aerodrome of disembarkation and of disembarkation without unnecessary suffering.

A veterinary inspector shall not certify a pony to be capable of being conveyed and disembarked if it is a mare and it is, in the inspector's opinion, heavy in foal, showing fullness of udder, or too old to travel: or if it is a foal, it is in his opinion too young to travel (Animal Health Act 1981, s.41(2)).

To comply with the requirements under s.41(1) of the 1981 Act, the owner or the person intending to ship the pony must supply to the Minister seven days before the date of shipment such evidence as may be required by the Minister, in respect of the use for which the pony is intended after export, and its value. Provided the evidence is satisfactory, a certificate to that effect will be issued. The certificate must be produced before the shipment, to the master of the vessel or the pilot of the aircraft.

A veterinary inspector may also mark any horse certified by him for identification purposes, and any person who tries to avoid the provisions of s.40 or s.41 by marking a horse with a prescribed mark or a mark similar that was calculated to deceive is guilty of an offence against the Act (s.45).

Under s.43 the Minister can make such orders as he feels are necessary to prohibit the export of ponies, unless they are rested and a suitable time is allowed for resting. The Minister can also make provisions for the cleansing and supervision of suitable premises and the bedding, food and water therein.

Under the Export of Horses (Protection) Order 1969, it is an offence for the master or pilot to allow a pony to be shipped unless he is given a certificate that the animal has been properly rested, or a licence of exemption from resting requirements from the Minister.

Section 42 of the Act makes it an offence to export a registered pony unless a certificate ('the export certificate') has been obtained from the secretary of the society in whose stud book the pony is registered. A registered pony is one who is registered in:

a) The Arab Horse Society Stud Book,
b) The National Pony Society Stud Book,
c) The British Palomino Society Stud Book, or
d) The British Spotted Horse and Pony Society Stud Book,

or in the stud book of any of the following native breed societies: English Connemara, Dales, Dartmoor, Exmoor, Fell, Highland, New Forest, Shetland or Welsh.

Exemptions

Racehorse enjoy certain exemptions under s.47 of the Animal Health Act 1981. Under that section, sections 40, 41and 46 do not apply to the shipment of any Thoroughbred horse which is certified in writing by a steward or the Secretary of the Jockey Club:

a) to have arrived in Great Britain not more than one month before the date of shipment for the purpose of being run in a race, or
b) to be shipped for the purpose of being run in a race, or
c) to be shipped in order to be used for breeding purposes.

The certificate must be delivered or produced in the same way as an inspector's certificate.

Ill and injured horses

Section 44 of the Animal Health Act gives an inspector the power to slaughter any animal which he has examined under s.40(1) and found to be in such physical condition that it would be cruel to keep it alive, or that it is permanently incapable of being walked without suffering. The slaughter must be carried out with a suitable mechanically operated instrument and no compensation will be paid to the owner.

Section 46 provides protection for injured horses, namely where an animal, whilst in transit, breaks a limb or is seriously injured so that it is incapable of being disembarked without cruelty, the master of the vessel will ensure that the animal is slaughtered forthwith and every vessel must carry an appropriate instrument to be approved by the Minister, with which to carry out that requirement. The duty rests upon the owner and master of the vessel to ensure that they are provided with the instrument and, if required by the inspector, must produce the instrument.

Diseases

The prevention and control of disease is most conveniently dealt with in this chapter, as it is most likely to affect persons involved in the importing and exporting of horses. The legislation dealing with this area of the law is consolidated in the Animal Health Act 1981. Among the diseases which relate to horses are: glanders or farcy, infectious equine anaemia, equine encephalomyelitis, African horse sickness, parasitic mange, equine virus abortion and epizootic lymphangitis (see the Infectious Diseases of Horses Order 1987 as amended in 1992 and 1995).

Section 1 of the Animal Health Act 1981 gives the Minister powers to make such orders as are thought fit to enable the execution of the Act and to prevent the spread of disease. The Act s.15(1), requires that any person who has in his possession or in his charge a horse affected by disease shall:

(i) as far as practicable keep the horse separate from unaffected horses, and

(ii) with all practicable speed, give notice of the fact of the horse's affliction to a constable of the area in which the horse is.

A police constable, having been so informed, should give that information forthwith to the relevant authority (s.15(3)). Any person who fails, without lawful authority or excuse, either to keep the animal separate or to give notice of the disease with all practicable speed will be guilty of an offence, the burden being on him to show that he *had* lawful authority or excuse.

Under s.16(1) of the 1981 Act, the Minister has the power to treat with serum or vaccine any horse which has been in contact with a diseased animal, is in an infected area, or has been exposed in some way to the infection.

The Minister is also empowered by s.17 to declare places and areas, for example stables and yards, infected areas. Further powers set out in s.23 include:

a) prohibiting or regulating the movement of animals and persons in or out of an infected area;
b) isolation or separation of animals in an infected place or area;
c) prohibiting or regulating the removal of carcasses, fodder, dung, etc. into, within or out of an infected place or area;
d) regulating the destruction, burial, disposal or treatment of carcasses;
e) regulating the disinfecting and cleansing of infected areas.

Under s.25 of the Act, the Minister is also given further powers to make orders in respect of movement of diseased animals or animals suspected of being diseased. These include regulations in respect of movement of:

(i)   the exposure of diseased or suspected animals in markets or farms or other places of sale;
(ii) the sending or carrying of diseased or suspected animals or other things likely to spread disease, including carriage by rail, water or air;
(iii) the carrying, leading or driving of diseased or suspected animals on the highway, etc.;
(iv) the placing or keeping of diseased or suspected animals on common or unenclosed lands, etc.

Section 28 of the Act also gives the Minister the power to seize diseased or suspected animals.

Chapter 7 RIDING ESTABLISHMENTS

This area divides into two distinct parts. First, the riding establishment itself and the laws that govern riding establishments, and second the duties and responsibilities that a proprietor of a riding establishment has under the law.

The Riding Establishment Acts

The law relating to riding establishments is almost entirely to be found in the Riding Establishments Acts of 1964 and 1970. These Acts are applicable to Scotland as well as England and Wales, but not to Northern Ireland. The purpose of the Acts is to ensure that some minimum standards are attained before a riding establishment can carry on business.

Licences
No one may keep a riding establishment except under the authority

of a licence granted by the relevant local authority (Riding Establishments Act 1964, s.1(1)). Section 6(1) of the Act defines a riding establishment as 'a place where horses are kept, either for letting out on hire for riding or for providing riding instruction in return for payment or both'. The Acts do not apply to all stables. For instance, a pure livery stable where no formal instruction is given would not require a licence, but an establishment where teaching was by demonstration only and the pupils never rode the horses, would still need a licence.

Under the Riding Establishments Act 1964, s.1(2), any person who is not disqualified from keeping a riding establishment, a dog, or a pet shop, from having the custody of animals or keeping boarding kennels, or who is not under eighteen, can obtain a licence. The Act further provides that the licence, if granted, must specify the premises where the business is to be carried on, and it is within the power of the local authority to impose conditions in respect of the operation of the establishment.

The local authority must have received and considered a report by its inspecting veterinary surgeon or practitioner in respect of an inspection of the relevant premises, including land; such inspection having taken place within the twelve months preceding the receipt by the local authority of the application, before any decision can be made on the granting of the licence. In considering the application, the local authority must have regard to specific matters which are set out in s.1(4) of the 1964 Act, namely:

a) Whether the person appears to them to be suitable and qualified, either by experience in the management of a riding establishment of horses or, being the holder of an approved certificate or by employing in the management of the riding establishment a person so qualified, to be the holder of such licence; and

b) the need for securing that:

   (i)   paramount consideration will be given to the condition of horses and that they will be maintained in good health, and are in all respects physically fit and that, in the case of a horse kept for the purpose of its being let out on hire for riding or a horse kept for the purpose of its being used in providing instruction in riding, the horse will be suitable for the purpose for which it is kept;

(ii) the feet of all animals are correctly trimmed and that, if shod, their shoes are properly fitted and in good condition;

(iii) there will be available at all times, accommodation for horses suitable as respects construction, size, number of occupants, lighting, ventilation, drainage and cleanliness, and that these requirements be complied with not only in the case of new buildings, but also in the case of buildings converted for use as stabling;

(iv) in the case of horses maintained at grass there will be available to them at all times during which they are so maintained, adequate pasture and shelter and water and that supplementary feeds will be provided as and when required;

(v)   horses will be adequately supplied with suitable food, drink, (and except in the case of horses maintained at grass, so long as they are so maintained) bedding material, and will be adequately exercised, groomed and rested and visited at suitable intervals;

(vi) all reasonable precautions will be taken to prevent and control the spread among horses of infections or contagious diseases and that veterinary, first aid equipment and medicines shall be provided and maintained in the premises;

(vii) appropriate steps will be taken for the protection and extrication of horses in the case of fire and, in particular, that the name, address, and telephone number of the licence holder or some other responsible person will be kept displayed in a prominent position on the outside of the premises and that the instructions as to the actions to be taken in the event of fire, with particular regard to the extraction of horses, will be displayed in a prominent position on the outside of the premises;

(viii) adequate accommodation will be provided for forage, bedding, stable equipment and saddlery.

These are wide-ranging matters for the local authority to consider and a person applying for a licence must give considerable thought to his arrangements if he wishes the licence to be granted. It is open to the local authority to specify any conditions in any licence granted, which it feels would be necessary or expedient to ensure that the matters to which it has to have regard can be adequately accommodated.

Where the grant of a licence is refused, there is a right of appeal to the Magistrates' Court, and there is also a right of appeal to the same court against any conditions which have been attached to the licence save for the conditions set out in s.1(4A) of the 1964 Act, namely that 'any horse found on inspection to need veterinary attention shall not be used until it has been certified fit, that there should be proper supervision for riders needing it, that the premises shall not be left in the charge of a person under the age of sixteen, that proper insurances shall be held and that a register of horse aged three years and under shall be kept'.

Under s.2 of the 1964 Act, the local authority can authorise, in writing, a person who is an officer of their or any other local authority, a veterinary surgeon or veterinary practitioner to inspect any premises in their area, that is:

(i) any premises where they have reason to believe someone is keeping a riding establishment;
(ii) any premises which has a current licence;
(iii) any premises for which an application has been made for a licence.

The person authorised under this section is entitled to enter the premises, on showing his authority, at all reasonable times to make inspection in order to make a report to the local authority in respect of an application for a licence, or to ascertain whether an offence has been or is being committed (Riding Establishments Act 1964, s.2).

Offences

Certain offences arise under the 1964 Act, the main ones being that it is an offence to keep a riding establishment without a licence and that a person who holds a licence is guilty of an offence if he in any way contravenes or does not comply with any condition of his licence. The offences are set out in s.3 of the 1964 Act and are as follows:

(i) Allowing a horse to be hired or used for riding instruction for payment or for demonstrations when it is in such a condition that riding it would be likely to cause unnecessary suffering to the horse.

(ii) Hiring a horse for instruction for payment or for demonstrations if the horse is aged three or under or if the horse is a mare heavy with foal or is a mare who has foaled within the preceding three months.

(iii) Supplying a horse with defective equipment which is likely to cause either suffering to the horse or accident to the rider.

(iv) Failing to provide curative care for a horse.

(v) Knowingly allowing any person disqualified from keeping stables to control or manage stables.

(vi) Concealing a horse to avoid its inspection.

It is also an offence to give false information in order to obtain a licence (s.3(2)).

The Act also sets out penalties in respect of offences under the Act. Offences under s.2(4) of the Act are dealt with in the Magistrates' Court and carry a maximum fine on level 3, presently £1,000. Offences under any other section are also dealt with in the Magistrates' Court and again carry a fine not exceeding level 3 or a term of imprisonment not exceeding three months, or both (s.4(2)).

On conviction under the Act, or under the Protection of Animals Act 1911, or the Protection of Animals (Scotland) Act 1912 or the Pet Animals Act 1951, or the Animal Boarding Establishments Act 1963, s.4(3) provides that the convicting court may cancel any licence held by the defendant under the Riding Establishments Act or may, whether or not such a licence is held, disqualify the defendant from keeping a riding establishment for any period the court thinks fit. Section 4(4) gives the court the power to suspend any order of disqualification pending an appeal.

The local authority has the power under s.5 of the Act to prosecute any offence under this Act, and no proceedings can be brought for an offence under s.1(9) save by the local authority, who can only institute proceedings after consideration of a veterinary report by an authorised surgeon or practitioner, which indicates that an offence has been committed.

Non-statutory Approval Schemes

In addition to the local authority licence, both the Association of British Riding Schools (ABRS) and the British Horse Society (BHS) operate national approval scheme for riding schools. In outline, these schemes are as follows.

The ABRS scheme

A high standard of care of the horses is expected and the instruction given must be well presented and correct in its content. The standards required of approval are set out in the Association's handbook and cover:

a) General appearance of the establishment, and in particular the stables and stalls.
b) The horses and ponies; care, grooming of and general condition.
c) Tack room and equipment; the condition, cleanliness and state of repair.
d) Facilities. This includes grazing and area for instruction.
e) Health and Safety standards must comply with current Health and Safety legislation and local council environmental targets.
f) Instruction; good sound instruction is expected at every level.

If, initially, a school does not come up to standard, advice will be given to help achieve approval. If the standard does not come up to an acceptable level the approval will not be considered. Once approval is given the Association expects the standard to be maintained and regular inspections are undertaken.

The Association has a disciplinary procedure which will consider every complaint made to the Association. It has to notify its findings and decisions to the complainant and the member complained of and the member has a right of appeal. The appeal will be considered by the Executive Committee. The member is entitled to appeal in person both before the Disciplinary Committee and the Executive Committee.

The BHS scheme

This scheme has two main objectives:

1. To lay down standards for riding establishments, to ensure that approved establishments meet the highest standards of instruction, safety and horse care.
2. To raise standards in riding establishments.

This approval scheme is not only for riding schools, but also livery yards and trekking centres. There are minimum standards expected in relation to stabling, bedding, manure storage, fencing, grazing land, worming programmes and shoeing.

There is also a Code of Conduct which sets out:

a) the responsibilities of the proprietor
b) emergency procedures
c) competence of the escort
d) duties of the escort
e) riders' clothing
f) conduct of the rides or treks
g) entering of unusual events in a report book.

Before BHS approval is granted, the riding establishment must show that it offers sound instruction in riding and stable management and that the animals, facilities and premises are properly looked after. Approval cannot be granted to a riding establishment unless it has a local authority licence. However, where an establishment offers training facilities, or is a livery yard or stud, provided it meets the Society's criteria for sound instruction it can be given approval even though a licence is not required. Where a livery yard seeks BHS approval it must provide clients with an acceptable written livery agreement and have effective isolation facilities.

The BHS inspectors will visit the approved establishments once every fifteen months unless there has been a complaint about the establishment, in which case more frequent visits will be made.

Duties and Responsibilities

Teaching

Although the niceties of the law are unlikely to be uppermost in the mind of the rider, nor possibly of the riding school proprietor, there is a contractual relationship between these parties. The proprietor is agreeing to teach the pupil to ride in return for payment. As was seen in Chapter 4 Buying and Selling, there can be implied and express terms of a contract of sale, both at common law and imposed by statute.

The Supply of Goods and Services Act 1982, s.13 provides that, in a contract for the supply of a service, where the supplier is acting in the course of a business, there is an implied term that the supplier will carry out the service with reasonable care and skill. In addition, it is also implied in the circumstance of teaching that the instructor has and will exercise such skills as are appropriate for his level of qualification, and that the horse provided is fit and sound, and that its nature is suitable for the experience and skill of the pupil. A further implied term is that the horse's tack is in a good and safe condition. Where an accident occurs and there is a breakdown in the relationship, the parties obviously have to look at the contract between them in the first instance. It may be that the contract does not cover that particular circumstance and it is, therefore, most likely that any action will be brought under the tort of negligence, which is dealt with in Chapter 2.

These responsibilities also apply to freelance instructors who are carrying on a business of teaching. All freelance instructors should carry proper insurance.

Hiring horses

Where a horse is merely hired and the proprietor does not undertake any teaching, there is an implied condition on the part of the proprietor that the horse and its equipment are suitable for the purpose for which they are required. It is incumbent upon the rider to specify precisely the purpose for which the horse is required. If the rider has an accident steeplechasing the horse when he has hired it for hacking, he is unlikely to have any redress against the proprietor.

It is also an implied term of this contract that the rider will take reasonable care of the horse for the whole time that it is in his possession and will return it at the end of the period of hire in the condition in which it left the yard. Even though payment is made, the hirer is, strictly speaking a bailee and has the responsibilities discussed earlier (see Chapter 1).

Livery yards

These may form an adjunct to a riding establishment or may stand on their own. In both cases contractual relationships exist between the parties and, where there is a breach of contract by the livery owner it is open to the yard owner to ask them to leave. Where there is a breach by the yard owner then damages may arise.

Both parties also owe a duty of care to each other. It is vitally important in this relationship that there is a written contract between the parties. A livery agreement should set out:

a) The basis of the livery e.g. full, combined, working or DIY.
b) What is expected by the yard owner of the livery owner and what the livery owner is paying for.
c) Rules as to the use of the yard's facilities.
d) Rules as to turnout.
e) Worming regime.
f) Basis of payment, e.g. whether in advance, by standing order.
g) Notice to be given by either side to terminate the agreement.
h) Rules as to insurance.
i) Rules as to inoculation, and whose responsibility this is.
j) Emergency procedures and contacts.

Chapter 8 RIGHTS OF WAY

One of the great pleasures derived from riding is the hack through pleasant countryside. Unfortunately, in a world where the use of motor cars is increasing, this pleasure is becoming more difficult and more dangerous for the horse rider. Bridleways are particularly important to the horse rider and it is vitally important that bridleways should be identified, used and preserved. This is now one of the major functions of the British Horse Society, which has a specific department to deal with access and rights of way, and also a network of bridleways officers around the regions.

The present Government has pledged that there will be a 'right to roam'. In order to enact this, the Countryside and Rights of Way Act was given the Royal Assent on 30 November 2000. The Act does not give the rights of access to the countryside to those on horseback, this being specifically excluded under Schedule 2(1), namely that the right of access to land applies only where a person is not accompanied by any animal, although there is the power to lift these restrictions. This may be only at certain times.

At the time of writing, only sections 81(2),(3), 103 and 104 are in force, with further sections coming into force on 30 January 2001. Included in these sections is s.65, which amends section 154 of the Highways Act 1980 which deals with the cutting or felling of over-hanging trees that are a danger to roads or footpaths. The amendment is to include trees, etc. which overhang the highway so as to endanger or obstruct the passage of horse riders.

There are two main proposed changes which will potentially affect the horse rider. One is the amendment to the Occupier's Liability Acts 1957 and 1984. The 1957 Act is to be amended to the effect that any person who goes onto land in exercise of his rights under the Countryside and Rights of Way Act 2000 will not be a visitor of the occupier of the premises. Under the 1984 Act, where a right under this new Act is exercisable, an occupier of the land will owe no duty of care in respect of a risk resulting from the existence of any natural feature of the landscape. If a person falls over a cliff whilst exercising his right of access on your land, you will not be liable. These provisions, contained in section 13, are not yet in force at the time of writing.

The second matter is that where, at present, the definitive map shows a road used as a public path, the public will, in future, have restricted byway rights which are:
a) a right of way on foot
b) a right of way on horseback or leading a horse
c) a right of way for vehicles other than mechanically propelled vehicles.

The duty to prepare maps, the publication thereof and the appeal procedure are contained in sections 4–6, which will be in force as of 30 January 2001. Other important sections for the horse rider are not in force at the time of writing. These include:
1. The redesignation of roads used as public paths (s.47).
2. Restricted bridleway rights (s.48).
3. Private rights over restricted byways (s.50).
4. Amendments relating to definitive maps and statements and restricted byways (s.51).
5. Extinguishment of unrecorded rights of way (s.53).
6. Excepted highways and rights of way (s.54).

7. Bridleway rights over ways shown as bridleways (s.55).
8. Cut-off date for extinguishment, etc. (s.56).
9. Creation, stopping up and diversion of highways (s.57).

There is no date for these sections to be enacted and at the time of writing there is no change in the law with which these sections deal.

What is a Bridleway?

At common law there are three types of highways. These are defined by the rights of passage over them. They are a footpath, a cartway or carriage way and a bridleway. A bridleway is defined as 'a highway over which the rights of passage are reduced by the exclusion of the right of passage with vehicles and sometimes driving cattle. A bridleway at common law includes a right of footway and there is a right to ride a bicycle along a bridleway'. A carriageway includes the rights of a footpath and bridleway.

A bridleway is defined by statute in section 329 of the Highways Act 1980 as 'a highway over which the public have the following, but no other rights of way, that is to say, a right of way on foot and a right of way on horseback or leading a horse with or without a right to drive animals of any description along the highway'. 'Horse' here includes pony, ass and mule. This definition also appears in the Road Traffic Regulation Act 1984 and the Wildlife and Countryside Act 1981.

Creation of bridleways

At common law, a bridleway is created when a legally competent person has dedicated to the public part of his land for the purpose of passage and that right of passage has been accepted for use. No formal act is necessary; acceptance can be inferred from use by the public. It is sufficient that the land has been used, without let or hindrance, for a length of time consistent with acceptance. The lack of definition of time has caused problems, but the Rights of Way Act 1932 (now repealed) set a time of twenty years use and enjoyment without interruption to give rise to the presumption of a highway, unless there is sufficient evidence to show there was no intention during that time to dedicate the way. This remains a statutory presumption (Highways Act 1980 s.31(1),(2)). It is open to the court to infer dedication where there is a shorter period of use. This will depend upon the facts of the particular case: in *R v Hudson* (1732) 2 Stra 909, four years was held to be insufficient time, whereas in *North London Railway Co. v St Mary Islington, Vestry* (1872) LT 672, eighteen months was held to be sufficient. In *Rugby Charitee Trustees v Merryweather* [1790] 11 East 375, six years was held to be sufficient and in *Jarvis v Dean* (1826) 3 Bing 447, eight years was sufficient.

The question whether or not there has been the dedication of a right of way is one of fact, and it will be determined on all the available evidence. The fact that the way has been used is merely evidence, it is not conclusive evidence. The user can, however, in the absence of any other evidence, raise a presumption of dedication. A presumption can always be rebutted. Where, however, the evidence of the user is satisfactory, dedication may be inferred even if the original owner cannot be traced. The burden of proving that there was no one who could have dedicated the way lies on the person who denies the alleged dedication. It is, therefore, open to the court to infer a bridleway from usage.

The court may also take into account the nature of the locality, i.e. where the way is situated and where it leads. A further consideration is how extensive the owner's acquiescence has been and in particular whether he has asserted his rights of ownership, but has not interfered with the public user.

The use of a bridleway must be as of right. The way must be open to all members of the public, not just a particular section, and must be a right that is always available. If there is any question of opening the way by force or seeking permission from time to time then a right of way cannot be inferred.

Where it is suggested that the use of the way has been interrupted, a single interruption can be of greater significance in deciding dedication, than many acts of enjoyment by the public. The closing of a way for one day a year is sufficient to negate dedication. Where a person using the way has been challenged and has turned back or has sought permission to use the way, this evidence of use is of no value and will undermine other evidence of the user. Where users have defied an owner when challenged and no legal proceedings have followed, the inference may be drawn that the owner knows that the way has been dedicated in the past.

Bars, notice boards declaring a private road and gates are also relevant to the question of dedication. Where these have been erected before the use began, there is unlikely to be an intention to dedicate. A locked gate is particularly strong evidence of no intention to dedicate, although an unlocked gate is not so clear, as there could be other reasons for having the gate – in particular to stop animals straying. The locking of a gate from time to time to prevent the straying of cattle has been held not to be a sufficient interruption to negate an intention to dedicate. (See *Lewis v Thomas* [1950] 1All ER 116).

Where a notice, inconsistent with dedication, has been erected and maintained and is visible to the user, then, if there is no evidence to the contrary, this will be sufficient for the court to say there is no evidence of dedication. If a notice falls into disrepair or is removed (not by the owner) then, if the owner has given notice to the appropriate council that there is not a dedicated way, this is again sufficient evidence to negate dedication unless, of course, there is any proof of a contrary intention.

Evidence that a way has been repaired at public expense is good evidence that it is a public right of way.

It is open to a landowner to deposit with the appropriate council a map of a scale of six inches to the mile or greater, together with a statement indicating the rights of way which are dedicated. Where there is a further statement within six years of the previous declaration or deposit, to the effect that no further ways have been dedicated, this will, provided there is no evidence of a contrary intention, be sufficient to negate any intention by the owner or his successors in title to dedicate any particular way as a highway.

An important factor in deciding whether or not there has been dedication of a bridleway is the evidence of reputation. This encompasses all evidence in respect of the bridleway. It can be in the form of statements, either orally or in writing from people with knowledge of the bridleway. When determining the question of dedication, a court or tribunal will always consider any map, plan or other history of the area. Any other documents which are relevant will be considered. A conviction relating to a way or perhaps a continuation in another district can also be admissible evidence (*R v Brightside Bierlow Inhabitants* (1849) 13 QB 933).

Where a road, which was originally a private way under an enclosure award for the use of specified people, is in fact used by the public, a subsequent dedication by the owner may be inferred. Similarly, if a public right of way is granted for a limited time by statute and the public continue to use it, a dedication by the landowner can be presumed. If a public right of way exists for certain purposes and the public use it for different purposes, dedication for the other purposes may be inferred, provided that no nuisance is caused by this changed or increased use.

New bridleways are created by statute under the Highways Act 1980. Section 25 enables a local authority to enter into a public path agreement with a person who has the power to dedicate a footpath or bridleway over land in the local authority area. Where such an agreement is made, it is the local authority's duty to take all necessary steps to ensure that the bridleway or footpath is dedicated in accordance with the agreement. Once this is done, the footpath or bridleway becomes maintainable at the public expense. The local authority must give notice of the dedication by publishing a notice in at least one local newspaper in the area.

Under section 26 of the Highways Act 1980, the local authority has the power to create a public path where, it appears to it, that there is a need for a footpath or bridleway and they are satisfied that it would be expedient for them to create the path. This is known as a public path order, which, once confirmed by the Secretary of State, creates a footpath or bridleway. Such confirmation is only necessary where the order is opposed. The local authority also has the power to make an order for the widening of an existing footpath or bridleway.

When a local authority is deciding whether the creation of the relevant path or way is expedient, it must consult any other local authorities in whose area the land concerned lies. The consideration for the local authority in deciding to create a new bridleway is the extent to which it would add to the convenience or enjoyment of a substantial section of the public or to the convenience of the residents of the area.

A public path creation order must be in the prescribed form. It must contain a map of not less than 1:2,500 or, if not available, the largest scale map which is available. The map must define the land over which the footpath or bridleway is created.

A public path creation order may be revoked or varied by further order.

A local authority also has the power to convert certain highways to footpaths or bridleways by extinguishing the right to use vehicles on them (Town and Country Planning Act 1990 s.249).

Section 30 of the Highways Act provides for the dedication of a bridleway by agreement with the parish or community council. This section is similar to s.25, but gives to the parish or community council the powers to enter into a dedication agreement with a person capable of dedicating land for the purpose of creating a bridleway.

Public rights

Where a highway has been created under an order, or expressly dedicated and accepted by the public as a particular kind of way, no question may arise as to the minimum rights of the public over it. Its rights cannot be diminished by non-use. Where a highway has been created from an inferred dedication it is a question of fact as to what traffic it was dedicated to. The right of the public to use bridleways has been extended by statute, irrespective of the way in which the highway itself was created originally. In general, apart from any local authority orders or by-laws, any member of the public has the right to ride a bicycle, not being a motor vehicle, on any bridleway, but when doing so a cyclist must give way to pedestrians and people on horseback.

The Clarification and Recording of Public Paths

Under the National Parks and Access to the Countryside Act 1949, a duty was imposed upon county councils to survey their areas to identify alleged public rights of way. Much of this Act has, however, now been repealed by the Wildlife and Countryside Act 1981. Section 53 of this Act continues to impose a duty to keep definitive maps and statements under continuous review. A definitive map and statement mean:

a) the latest revised map and statement prepared in definitive form for the area under the National Parks and Countryside Act 1949 s.33 (now repealed) or

b) where no such map and statement have been prepared for the area, the original map and statement under s.33; or

c) where no such map and statement have been prepared, the map and statement prepared for the Wildlife and Countryside Act 1981.

Under the Wildlife and Countryside Act 1981 s.56, the definitive map and statement are conclusive as to the particulars contained in them to this extent:

1. where a map shows a footpath, the map shall be conclusive evidence that there was at the relevant date a highway as shown on the map, and that the public had thereover a right of way on foot, but without prejudice to any question whether the public had at that date any other right of way other than that right;

2. where the map shows a bridleway, the map shall be conclusive evidence that there was at the relevant date a highway as shown on the map, and that the public had thereover at that date a right of way on foot and a right of way on horseback or leading a horse, so however that this paragraph shall be without prejudice to any question whether the public had at that date any right of way other than those rights;

3. where the map shows a byway open to all traffic, the map shall be conclusive evidence that there was at the relevant date a highway as shown on the map, and that the public had thereover at that date a right of way for vehicular and all other kinds of traffic;

4. where the map shows a road used as a public path, the map shall be conclusive evidence that there was at the relevant date a high way as shown on the map, and that the public had thereover at that date a right of way on foot and a right of way on horseback

or leading a horse, so however that this paragraph shall be without prejudice to any question whether the public had at that date any right of way other than those rights;

5. where by virtue of the foregoing paragraphs the map is conclusive evidence, as at any date, as to a highway shown thereon, or any particulars contained in the statement as to the position or width thereof shall be conclusive evidence as to the position or width thereof at that date, and any particulars so contained as to limitations or conditions affecting the public rights of way shall be conclusive evidence that at the said date the said right was subject to those limitations or conditions, but without prejudice to any other question whether the right was subject to any other limitations or conditions at that date.

The expression 'road used as a public path' should no longer be used (Wildlife and Countryside Act 1981 s.54 as amended).

The surveying authority must keep copies of all maps, statements and orders modifying such maps and statements. These must be available free of charge at all reasonable hours and in more than one place.

It is the duty of the surveying authority to make such modifications to the map and statement as are necessary in respect of the occurrence of certain events, and they must thereafter keep the map and statement under continuous review to enable them to modify the map and statement (s.53(2)(a),(b)). The events referred to are as follows:

a) the coming into operation of any enactment or instrument, or any other event whereby:
 (i) a highway shown or required to be shown in the map and statement has been authorised to be stopped up, diverted, widened or extended;
 (ii) a highway shown or required to be shown in the map and statement as a highway of a particular description has ceased to be a highway of that description; or
 (iii) a new right of way has been created over land in the area to which the map relates, being a right of way such that the land over which the right subsists is a public path;

b) the expiration, in relation to any way in the area to which the map relates, of any period, such that the enjoyment by the public of the way during that period raises a presumption that the way has been dedicated as a public path;

c) the discovery by the authority of evidence which (when considered with all the other evidence available to them) shows:

  (i) that a right of way which is not shown on the map and statement subsists or is reasonably alleged to subsist over the land in the area to which the map relates, being a right of way to which this part applies;

  (ii) that a highway shown in the map and statement as a highway of a particular description ought to be shown there as a highway of a different description; or

  (iii) that there is no public right of way over land shown in the map and statement as a highway of any description, or any other particulars contained in the map and statement require modification.

This section is important to riders because, if they can produce evidence to the surveying authority that a particular path has been used as a bridleway, but not marked as such, then there is clearly a duty on the authority to consider the evidence and if satisfied to act upon it.

The term 'road used as a public path' has caused difficulty in the past, because s.27(3) of the 1949 Act defined a road used as a public path as being 'a highway, other than a public path, used by the public mainly for the purposes for which footpaths or bridleways are so used'. The 1949 Act and later the Countryside Act 1968 said that these should be reclassified and under this special review Kent County Council tried to downgrade a road used as a public path into a footpath. This culminated in the case of *R v Secretary of State for the Environment, ex parte Hood* [1975].

Kent County Council had prepared a definitive map of the relevant area under the 1949 Act. When the map was prepared, however, the public right of way over the path in question was not clear, in that it was not known whether the right of way included a right of way on foot. As there was no other right of way under the Act, the path was shown on the definitive map as a road used as a public path. Under s.32(4)(b) of the 1949 Act, there was a conclusive presumption that the public had the right of way on horseback or leading a horse over the path. Under the Countryside Act 1968, the County Council undertook a special review of 'roads used as public paths' and, at the time of that review, there was no new evidence to show whether or not the path was subject to a right of passage on or with horses. The County Council, therefore, proposed that the path should be classified as a footpath. This proposal was confirmed by the Secretary of State for the Environment. The appellant, supported by the British Horse Society, applied for an order of *certiorari* (a civic remedy) to quash the decision but the application was refused.

The BHS appealed to the Court of Appeal on the basis that, because the path was conclusively presumed to be one over which the public had rights of bridleway as well as footway, it should be reclassified as a bridleway. The Court of Appeal allowed the appeal, holding that, where on a special review, a path which had formerly been classed as a 'road used as a public path' could not be reclassified as 'byway open to all traffic', the authority responsible for preparing the definitive map was bound by the presumption under s.32(4)(b) of the 1949 Act. In the absence of new evidence that there was no right of bridleway, the County Council were bound to classify the path as a bridleway and that order was made.

This was an important case because it meant that a right of way could not be downgraded without the production of new evidence as to its use. The sections referred to in the judgment have now been repealed by the Wildlife and Countryside Act 1981, and replaced by section 54 (dealing with the duty to reclassify roads) and section 56 (dealing with the presumption that a definitive map is conclusive) of that Act.

The definitive map does not necessarily remain conclusive evidence of a particular right of way forever. There is provision for reviews. In *Suffolk v Mason* [1979] AC 705 Lord Diplock said at page 714:

> On a revision, entries on the definitive map which require modification as a result of events that have occurred since the date of the last revision may be modified accordingly. Among the subsequent events which call for a

modification of an entry is the discovery by County Council of new evidence, which if it had been known to them at the time of the last revision, would have resulted in their being required to enter it on the definitive map as a highway of a different description. So an entry made by mistake would, if the Act were administered in accordance with its terms, endure for a maximum of five years after the error was discovered.

Despite the above decision a different decision was made in *Rubinstein v Secretary of State for the Environment* [1988] JPL 485. In that case, two members of the Ramblers Association applied to the High Court as persons aggrieved by an order made under section 53 and confirmed by the Secretary of State. A footpath was shown as a right of way on a definitive map published on 21 May 1959. The Inspector found that on the relevant date, 1 January 1953, there was on the evidence no right of way, and that, therefore, the path should not have been included on the plan. Taylor J held that the decision of the Inspector was wrong and that the ramblers were correct in saying that under sections 53 and 56, once a footpath is shown on a definitive map, it is not permissible to remove it, even where there is evidence that it should not have originally been included.

This decision, whilst being of assistance where bridleways were shown, could nevertheless have been very unhelpful if only a footpath was shown where there was evidence that there was in fact a bridleway. It is clear from the wording of the statute that Parliament did not intend maps to be definitive where there was evidence to show that the map could be wrong.

The anomaly of this decision was dealt with in *R v Secretary of State for the Environment ex-parte Simms and R v Secretary of State for the Environment ex-parte Burrows* [1990] 3WLR 1070. In these two cases, which were heard together, it was held that on a proper construction of sections 53 and 56 of the Wildlife and Countryside Act 1981, a definitive map was conclusive evidence that a particular way existed only until a subsequent revision of the map, when it could be modified to rectify any mistake which had been made; that, if evidence became available which indicated that a footpath had been incorrectly classified as a bridleway or that a bridleway which had not previously existed had been erroneously included in the map, the bridleway could be reclassified or deleted from the map under section 53(3)(c). *Rubenstein v Secretary of State for the Environment* was specifically overruled.

There is clearly a duty upon the local authority to review the definitive map and to revise and rectify it where necessary. If the evidence on a map is wrong it can be changed and it is, therefore, important for riders who use bridleways to be aware of this, as their evidence could be important if a map is wrong.

Two other decisions of note are *R v Secretary of State for the Environment ex-parte Riley* [1989] and *R v Isle of Wight C.C. ex-parte O'Keefe* (1989) which deal, respectively, with the reclassification of a bridleway and a procedural point in respect of a modification order.

Proper Use of Bridleways and Associated Land

It is important that riders ensure that any right of way is not abused. A bridleway is only dedicated to the public for passage. 'Passage' is not strictly limited to its ordinary meaning; riders are able to stop for a reasonable period of time to admire the view or to rest their horses. However, continually passing and re-passing on the same stretch for long periods of time might be considered an abuse of the right. It may be tempting to put up jumps on a bridleway, but, apart from hindering passage, it may also be in breach of s.131A of the Highways Act 1980 as amended by the Rights of Way Act 1990. This section also makes it an offence to disturb the surface of a bridleway so as to render it inconvenient for the exercise of a public right of way.

This also raises the question of obstructions. Locked gates or a fence may obstruct a bridleway. It may be that those obstructions are illegal. However, before taking action, a rider should first consult the statement attached to the definitive map, as conditions may have been attached to the dedication. The second action should be to check whether permission has been applied for in respect of the obstruction, as the local authority does have the power to give permission for gates to be erected in certain circumstances (Highways Act 1980, s.147). It is important that riders do make these checks to ensure that the bridleways remain open because, if a landowner is consistently improperly blocking a bridleway, it may be possible to obtain an injunction to restrain him. The 1980 Act also makes provision under s.145 for enlargement or removal of gates and, under s.14, imposes a duty on the owner of the land to maintain gates and other structures in a safe condition.

The Rights of Way Act 1990 strikes a balance between landowners and the users of rights away by amending the Highway Act 1980. Apart from interference with the surface of the right of way, the amended s.134 of the 1980 Act allows farmers to plough land over which a bridleway runs, in certain circumstances. There is a duty to make good the surface of the right of way and to indicate the line of the path, within a certain period of time as stipulated in the Act. Further amendments cover the planting of crops, to ensure that rights of way are not interfered with or encroached upon, and the granting of permission to farmers to carry out excavation which may disturb a bridleway, providing it is reasonable and an application has been made to the highway authority.

Section 59 of the Wildlife and Countryside Act prohibits the occupier of a field crossed by a right of way from permitting a bull to be at large in the field, unless the bull is under ten months old or is not of a recognised dairy breed and is at large with cows or heifers. This an offence which is triable summarily and subject to a fine not exceeding level three on the standard scale.

Signposts

Section 27 of the Countryside Act 1968 gives the highway authority the power to erect and maintain signposts along any bridleway in its area after it has consulted with the owner or occupier of the land. The signposts must be erected where the bridleway leaves a metalled road and show, where appropriate, where the bridleway leads and the distance to any places named on the signpost. If, after consultation with the parish or community council, the highway authority is satisfied that a signpost in a particular place is not necessary, it need not erect one. In exercising its power, the highway authority must put up signposts, which in its opinion, will assist riders, who are unfamiliar with the locality, to follow the bridleway.

Provided the highway authority consents, any person is entitled to erect and maintain signposts along the bridleway, and it is an offence to destroy or deface any signpost erected along a bridleway (Highways Act 1980,s.131(2)).

Trespassing

Even the most diligent rider may get lost out hacking and trespass on another's land and he should, therefore, be aware of any possible consequences.

Trespass is the unlawful entry by one person on to land in the possession of another. Entry, however, does not necessarily mean physical entry: allowing your horse to eat the neighbour's plants or vegetables over the fence may be trespass. Generally, however, the rider trespassing will do so by riding his horse onto the land. Unfortunately, not all bridleways are signposted in the proper fashion and the rider may find himself unwittingly trespassing after taking a wrong turning. Even though this is unintentional, it is still trespassing. In certain circumstances, namely long use, if a bridleway is badly signposted or obstructed and it has become the practice to take a route onto adjoining land, this may not be trespass. Where the rider goes intentionally onto someone else's land, then he is clearly trespassing. It can, however, be a defence to an action for trespass, that the rider arrived on the land not by his own actions. For example, if a horse bolts onto the land in question, then the rider cannot be sued for trespass. Trespass must be voluntary.

A landowner must first request the trespasser to leave his land. A trespasser who refuses to go can then be physically ejected, but only by the use of reasonable force. If a landowner does not ask a trespasser to leave before using force, or if he uses unnecessary force, he may find himself liable for assault. The landowner can sue for damages for trespass and, where a rider consistently trespasses, the landowner can apply for an injunction preventing the rider from coming on to his land.

It is, perhaps, whilst out hunting that a rider is most likely to trespass and there is no doubt that entering on to another person's land without his consent whilst hunting is a trespass (*Paul v Summerhayes* (1878)). The Master of Hounds is always at risk of his hounds trespassing and in *League Against Cruel Sports v Scott and Others* [1985] it was held that a Master of Hounds is vicariously liable for the acts and omissions, not only of the hunt servants and agents, but also of the mounted followers. It is, therefore, important that followers do not trespass on to prohibited land, as they not only risk being sued themselves, but may also cause the Master to be sued as well.

In this case, however, it was also held that a Master will only be liable for trespass if, in deliberately taking hounds in pursuit of a quarry, knowing that there is a risk that they would trespass, he in effect intended to cause the hounds to enter the prohibited land. He would also be liable if, by his negligence in controlling the pack, he failed to prevent the hounds from entering the land. It follows, therefore, that if a Master insisted upon hunting in an area where he knew it was virtually impossible to prevent hounds from trespassing, his indifference to the risk of trespass could be seen as an intention to trespass. The judge went on to hold that it was a question of fact as to whether the conduct of the hunt amounted to trespass.

In connection with hunting, there have been a number of incidents when people have trespassed on private property in an attempt to disrupt a hunt, and legislation has been enacted to deal with this. Under the Public Order Act 1986 s.39, if a senior police officer reasonably believes that two or more persons have entered land as trespassers and are present there with the common purpose of residing there for any period, that reasonable steps have been taken by or on behalf of the occupier to ask them to leave and:

a) that any of those persons has caused damage to property on the land or used threatening, abusive or insulting words or behaviour towards the occupier, a member of his family or an employee or an agent of his; or

b) that those persons have between them brought twelve or more vehicles on to the land;

he may direct that those persons, or any of them, leave the land. If a person knowing that such a direction has been given which applies to him:

a) fails to leave the land as soon as reasonably practicable; or
b) having left enters the land again as a trespasser within the period of three months beginning with the day on which the direction was given,

he commits an offence. A constable who reasonably suspects that a person is committing an offence under these provisions may arrest him without warrant.

It is a defence for a person charged with this offence to show:

a) that the original entry on the land was not as a trespasser; or
b) that he had a reasonable excuse for failing to leave the land as soon as reasonably practicable or, as the case may be for entering the land again as a trespasser.

Chapter 9 ROAD TRAFFIC LAW

Certain aspects of the Highway Code which may be relevant to horse riders were discussed earlier in Chapter 2 Negligence. Overall, Road Traffic Law affects several areas of horse ownership. It is a complex and vast area of the law. This chapter is intended to highlight those issues most likely to affect the horse owner in their daily equestrian pursuits, and assist those advising them when problems arise.

The principle sources of legislation are the various Road Traffic Acts and Construction and Use Regulations. In addition, there exist ancient and obscure offences principally related to horses and carriages. This is unsurprising given that the motor car has replaced the horse as the universal means of transport of the modern era. Perhaps the new millennium will herald a return to the ecologically safe and renewable resource of the horse and carriage!

The Use of Motor Vehicles and Trailers

When towing a horse trailer, or driving a lorry that carries a horse, the owner and/or driver are subject to a varied array of duties and obligations. Breaches of them can have very serious consequences.

Trailers

A trailer is not subject to an MOT test. Nonetheless, it must be in a safe condition. Particular attention should be paid to its tyres, brakes and lights, as defects to any of these contravene Construction and Use Regulations.

The trailer must display the registration number of the towing vehicle. The weight of the trailer, either laden or unladen, must not exceed the permitted weight for the towing vehicle. This will differ depending upon whether the trailer has its own independent braking system or is an unbraked trailer. It is advisable to know the unladen weight of the trailer and the individual weights of the horses/ponies to be carried.

If the driver of the towing vehicle passed their driving test after 1 January 1997, a separate test is required to tow any trailer weighing over 750 kg. This will almost certainly include all horse trailers.

The maximum speed limit for towing a trailer on motorways and dual carriageways is 60 mph, and upon other roads 50 mph, subject to any lesser maximum governing a particular stretch of road. Whether it is advisable to tow a laden trailer at any speed approaching that maximum is a matter of debate. Speeding with horses on board could, in certain circumstances, amount to either dangerous or careless driving.

The right hand lane of a motorway with three or more lanes must not be used when towing a trailer.

All motor vehicles must be covered by a minimum of third party insurance. All such policies should insure in respect of any liabilities incurred by the use of the trailer when in tow to the insured vehicle (see ss.143–145 Road Traffic Act 1988). *This does not extend insurance cover to an unhitched trailer and may not cover theft even when hitched. Separate insurance for the trailer is highly advisable.*

A trailer must not be left on a road at night without being lit.

Lorries

Any lorry exceeding 7.5 tonnes is classified as a Heavy Goods Vehicle. This has implications. A separate driving licence is required, for which twenty-one is the minimum age limit. An annual test of the vehicle is mandatory and is governed by Goods Vehicles (Plating and Testing) Regulations 1988. Using or permitting the use of the lorry without the relevant test having been successfully completed, is an offence.

For those who passed their driving test after 1 January 1997, who wish to drive a medium-sized lorry of between 3.5 and 7.5 tonnes, a separate test is required. The minimum age for this is eighteen.

Dangerous or careless driving

The distinction to be drawn between dangerous and careless driving is a qualitative one, grounded essentially upon the standard of driving displayed. It is a matter of fact and degree. Self-evidently it is dangerous driving that is the more serious, and all the more so if it causes the death of another.

The offences of causing death by dangerous driving and dangerous driving were created by ss.1 and 2 of the Road Traffic Act 1988 and 1991. Dangerous driving is committed where the vehicle is driven in a manner which falls way below the standard expected of a competent and careful driver, and in circumstances in which it would be obvious to such a careful and competent driver that driving in that way would be dangerous. A conviction leads to an automatic disqualification from driving and a prison sentence may be imposed if the dangerous driving warrants it (maximum six months on summary conviction, two years upon indictment). Where the dangerous driving has caused the death of another it is a grave offence carrying the maximum of ten years imprisonment. Save in exceptional circumstances, a dangerous driver who kills someone else goes to prison.

Careless driving is defined by s.3 of the 1988 Act as 'departing from the standard of a reasonable, prudent and competent driver in all the circumstances of the case'. It is a lower test than that set for ss.1 and 2. A conviction may lead to a disqualification, but will certainly involve an endorsement upon the driver's licence of between

3 and 9 points. The sliding scale reflects the fact that there can be a wide difference in seriousness in this offence.

Driving whilst under the influence of drink or drugs

In this context, the law uses the term 'drink' to imply alcoholic drink. Section 11 of the Road Traffic Act 1988 defines 'drug' as: 'includes any intoxicant other than alcohol'. 'Intoxicant' describes any substance that affects the self-control of the human body, and therefore includes prescriptive drugs.

It is an offence to :

1. Drive or attempt to drive a mechanically propelled vehicle while unfit to drive through drink or drugs.
2. Be in charge of a mechanically propelled vehicle while unfit to drive through drink or drugs.
3. Drive or attempt to drive a motor vehicle on a road or other public place after consuming so much alcohol that the proportion of it in the driver's breath, blood or urine exceeds the prescribed limit*.
4. Be in charge of a motor vehicle on a road or other public place after consuming alcohol so that the proportion of it in the person's breath, blood or urine exceeds the prescribed limit*.
5. Without reasonable excuse, fail to supply specimens of breath, blood or urine for analysis.

*The following are the limits set out by UK law:
35 microgrammes of alcohol in 100 millilitres of breath, or
80 milligrammes of alcohol in 100 millilitres of blood, or
107 milligrammes of alcohol in 100 millilitres of urine.

Disqualification is obligatory, and in gross or persistent cases a prison sentence may follow.

As with dangerous driving, there is the aggravated offence where drunken driving leads to the death of another. The offence is set out in s.3A of the Road Traffic Acts 1988 and 1991. Where the driver causes death by careless driving (see above) and is unfit through drink or drugs, or over the prescribed limit, the penalties are the same as causing death by dangerous driving. The offence may well be easier to prove, but the likelihood of a substantial prison sentence is just the same.

The Use of Horse and Carriage

In the main, the riding of horses and the driving of carriages are not covered by Road Traffic Act legislation. It follows, therefore, that some of the following offences can be committed even though not on a road or in a public place. In this regard, certain ancient powers are more extensive than those of the Road Traffic Acts.

If you ride a horse or drive a horse and carriage whilst drunk you commit an offence under s.12 of the Licensing Act 1872. The test for proving this offence is higher than for drink-driving. The prosecution must prove that the rider/driver was drunk, not merely under the influence of alcohol. There is no provision for breath, blood or urine tests. It is likely that the alleged offender would be visited by the police surgeon who would conduct a number of tests and observations in order determine whether the person was drunk or not. The offence carries a fine, or imprisonment of up to one month.

The 'wanton and furious driving or racing' of a horse and carriage is an offence under s.35 of the Offences Against the Person Act 1861. This section extends to 'other wilful misconduct or wilful neglect'. However, these features must cause some bodily harm to someone for the offence to be complete. This matter can only be tried upon indictment unless committed by a youth. The courts appear to treat this as a crime of basic intent. It carries a maximum of two years imprisonment.

A horse should not be ridden or led on a pavement (s.72 Highways Act 1835).

If a horse strays onto the highway its keeper is liable under section 155 of The Highways Act 1980 (see also Chapters 1 and 3).

The Highways Act 1835 regulates the use of horse drawn carriages upon the road. Of particular relevance, it prohibits :

causing damage to person or goods,

not being in proper control of the horses drawing the carriage,

preventing others from passing,

allowing the carriage to obstruct the highway.

If the carriage is used for any form of commercial hire (for example, weddings), pre-1930 Hackney cab regulations may apply. Consideration should also be given to any local by-laws.

The Town Police Causes Act 1847 prohibits (amongst many obscure matters) on a thoroughfare:

exposing for show or sale a horse (save in a lawfully appointed market),

shoeing a horse (except in the case of an accident),

cleaning, dressing, training or breaking any horse,

repairing a carriage, save in an emergency.

Finally, it is always advisable for all riders to wear a proper riding hat and body protector. For riders under the age of fourteen, the wearing of a riding hat/helmet which complies with the current regulations is mandatory. The hat/helmet *must* be fastened securely (Horses (Protective Headgear for Young Riders) Regulations 1992). (See also The Law of Negligence and Horse Owners in Chapter 2.)

This list is not intended to be a comprehensive guide. In particular cases, reference will have to be made to more detailed and specialised works. However, consideration of the contents of this chapter, the Highway Code, the British Horse Society tests/guidelines and above all common sense, should keep a competent rider on the right side of the law!

Chapter 10 PREMISES FOR HORSE-KEEPING

The ideal of most horse owners is to have a house with stables and land attached, either as a freehold property or on a very long lease (i.e. 999 years). Such ideals are, however, not always attainable and other options, such as shorter term leasing, and their legal consequences are considered here in general terms.

Purchasing

Generally speaking, the purchase of premises on which to keep horses is subject to the same irritations and problems as any ordinary purchase. However, some extra care must be taken in respect of any restrictions upon use which may attach to the land. There may be restrictive covenants, to which the property is subject, limiting certain forms of use. This is of particular concern to persons wishing to purchase a property for business purposes and, when dealing with this type of purchase, both the estate agent and the solicitor involved should be made aware of the uses for which the premises are required.

In addition to any restrictions on use, particular care should also be taken in respect of rights of way over land. A problem may arise if there is a right of way through areas where horses are kept, particularly if such right is not merely for persons on foot, but also for driven animals or even vehicles. Apart from these rights, if the land or premises are isolated, it may be important to ensure that there are rights over neighbouring property to enable electricity and water to be provided, and that there are also drainage rights. Of additional importance, particularly, so far as the land itself is concerned, is to establish who is responsible for fencing the land.

Planning permission

If the intention is to use the property for a business, such as a riding establishment, for which it has not been used before, planning permission for change of use will be required, and the new venture will probably be subject to business rates.

Any carrying out of building on land, or the making of any material change in the use of buildings or land constitutes development and will require permission. Permission, therefore, will be needed for stables although, under s.55(1)(2)(d) of the Town and Country Planning Act 1990, where the use of the buildings or other land is within the curtilage of a dwelling house for any purpose incidental to the enjoyment of the dwelling house as such, it does not constitute development and, therefore, permission is not required. This means that, generally speaking, if one wishes to construct a stable or stables within the garden or yard of a property, then permission will not be required as it is not considered as development within the Act. Potential problems may arise over 'purpose incidental to the enjoyment of the property' and what constitutes 'the curtilage'. If the curtilage or area of the property were large enough to build a number of stables which were to be used for business purposes, then permission would be required as this would not be a use incidental to the residential enjoyment of the property. If the dwelling house is a listed building then, under the Town and Country Planning General Development Order 1988, construction of a stable would not be permitted development.

Section 55(2)(e) of the Town and Country Planning Act states that 'the use of land for agriculture or forestry and the use for any of those purposes of any building occupied together with the land so used will not constitute development and planning permission will not be required', although there may be certain circumstances where permission is required under the Town and Country Planning General Development Order 1988 and specialist advice should be sought.

Section 336(1) defines agriculture, for the purposes of the Town and Country Planning Act 1990, as including 'horticulture, fruit growing, seed growing, dairy farming, the breeding and keeping of livestock (including any creature kept for the production of food, wool, skins or fur, or for the purpose of its use in the farming of land), the use of land as grazing land, meadow land, osier land, market gardens and nursery grounds, and the use of land for woodlands where that use is ancillary to the farming of the land for other agricultural purposes'.

Horses are not included in the definition of agriculture unless it can be shown that the horses are kept purely for farming purposes. This is a narrow distinction and in *Belmont Farms v Minister of Housing and Local Government* (1962) 60 LGR 319 it was held that this did not extend to the breeding and keeping of horses as showjumpers. The breeding and keeping of horses must be for use in the farming of land. Grazing land which is part of the definition of agriculture under s.336(1) does, however, include the land used for grazing racehorses, ponies and point-to-point horses (*Sykes v Secretary of State for the Environment* [1981] 42 P & CR 19).

It follows, therefore, that permission is likely to be required to place anything on land which is used by horses, whether stables, an all-weather arena, or a field shelter. The granting of such permission is likely to include permission for change of use if the land had previously been used for agricultural purposes. A possible exception to this is the mobile field shelter although, where there is a permanent concrete base, there may be an argument as to the permanency of the building.

When seeking permission it is always advisable to work with the local authority and to follow accepted guidelines as to the construction of stables, whether from the British Horse Society or the Countryside Commission.

Tenancies

If the purchase of suitable premises is not feasible, then renting in various forms is an alternative. Prima facie, any tenancy will, of course, give the tenant exclusive occupation and the right to exclude anyone, including the landlord (unless, as often happens, the landlord reserves to himself certain rights to come on to the land from time to time).

The law relating to landlord and tenant is a complex amalgam of the common law and many statutory enactments. What is set out here is simply a framework setting out the common forms of tenancy. As with other subjects covered herein, there are authoritative works of reference, such as Hill and Redman's *Landlord and Tenant* and William Woodfall's *Law of Landlord and Tenant*.

Fixed term tenancies

A fixed term tenancy is, as the name suggests, a tenancy for a fixed period of time. Theoretically, the tenancy only comes to an end at the expiration of that time and there is no need for a Notice to Quit. In practice, to comply with certain statutory provisions, it is often necessary to serve a notice of some description, for example a landlord's notice under s.25 of the Landlord and Tenant Act 1954.

This type of tenancy may be a long-term commitment which obliges the tenant not only to pay rent but also, for example, to pay for repairs to the building as well as the cost of insuring it. The terms of the lease should, therefore, be studied carefully as there may be restrictions on use as well as covenants preventing assigning or subletting. Often there will be forfeiture clauses, which enable a landlord to repossess the premises if the rent is in arrears (or indeed, if any other covenant in the lease is broken), although a landlord will usually have to serve notice requiring the breach to be remedied before he can forfeit a lease in such circumstances (Law of Property Act 1925, s.146)).

In addition to any right to forfeit, the landlord may also bring an action for arrears of rent, or he may make use of the ancient remedy of distress. Although distress for rent was described by Lord Denning in *Abingdon Rural District Council v O'Gorman* (1968) as 'an archaic remedy which had largely fallen into disuse', it does arise from time to time and merits a brief reference.

Distress occurs where the landlord enters onto the premises and takes possession of goods or cattle to the value of the rent owed. In the first instance they are held as a pledge, but after a period (which may be only five days) they can be sold. There are certain exemptions for some farm animals but, in general terms, a tenant's horses are able to be distrained upon (i.e. eventually sold to pay any rent outstanding).

Periodic tenancies

A periodic tenancy continues automatically from period to period until it is determined by a Notice to Quit. The periods generally speaking will be weekly, monthly, quarterly or yearly, although it is open to the parties to stipulate any period they wish.

A periodic tenancy can be created either by express agreement or by implication. If a person occupies land with the owner's permission, and is not a licensee, and there is no agreement as to how long he should remain, and rent is paid and accepted, and is expressed or calculated as a yearly sum, then it is likely that a yearly tenancy will be created. When the rent is expressed in other ways, (e.g. weekly, monthly or quarterly), then this is likely to be the period of the tenancy. Where, however, the tenant remains in possession due to a statutory right to occupy (e.g. under the Rent Act 1977 or Part II of the Landlord and Tenant Act 1954), or because he is holding over at the end of the lease, then simply because rent is accepted in a particular way does not necessarily give rise to a periodic tenancy.

Any agreement can be made as to the manner of ending the tenancy but, in the absence of agreement, a yearly tenancy will be determined on giving at least six months notice which must expire at the end of a complete year of a tenancy. Quarterly, weekly and monthly tenancies are determinable on giving notice of one full period, expiring at the end of a complete period of the tenancy.

Tenancy at will

This type of tenancy arises where a tenant is occupying land with the owner's consent, provided the tenancy can be ended at any time by either party. It can, however, also be created by implication in certain circumstances, usually where a tenant occupies with permission of the landlord, but does not pay rent. As soon as rent is paid and accepted on a regular basis, some sort of periodic tenancy is created. It is an interesting point that a tenancy at will is not protected by the Landlord and Tenant Act 1954, Part II.

Residential tenancies

Although it is possible that some tenants still hold their property governed by earlier Acts, the Housing Act 1988 and the Rent Act 1977 are the two main statutes covering rented residential accommodation. In simple terms, if the tenancy of a dwelling house was granted before 15 January 1989 then it is covered by the Rent Act 1977; after that time the Housing Act 1988 is the relevant statute.

Under the Rent Act 1977, the tenant of a dwelling house became a 'protected tenant'. If, for example, the landlord and tenant agreed that the tenancy was going to be a monthly tenancy, that did not mean that the landlord could evict the tenant at the end of a month. If a landlord served a Notice to Quit terminating the tenancy, all that notice did was to convert the protected tenancy into what was called a 'statutory tenancy'. It was not easy to evict a statutory tenant; even arrears of rent did not oblige the court to make an order for possession; it merely gave the court a discretion to do so. Furthermore, a protected tenant was entitled to ask the Rent Officer to fix a 'fair rent' for the property. Fair rents were usually significantly lower than the open market rent.

The 1988 Housing Act marked a significant move by Parliament from favouring the tenant to favouring the landlord. It was described by the Secretary of State for the Environment as '...a major step forward in improving the opportunities, choices and conditions of all those who rent rather than buy their own homes' and by the

Shadow Spokesman on the Environment as heralding '...the return of Rachmanism, harassment, extortion, and probably criminal activities in the housing market'.

The 1988 Act creates two types of tenancy:
1. the assured tenancy (which is a watered-down version of the old protected tenancy) and
2. the assured shorthold tenancy.

Whilst the assured tenancy does provide the tenant with some protection, it is significantly less than existed hitherto and new grounds for possession have been introduced (for example, Ground 6: the landlord wishes to demolish or reconstruct the dwelling). Furthermore, arrears of rent, in certain circumstances, now provides a mandatory basis for possession and even persistent delay in paying rent gives the court discretion to order possession. The rights to succession to the tenancy by a widow or a member of the deceased's family are curtailed.

The assured shorthold tenancy, on the other hand, gives the tenant little security. Originally, the 'default' position was an assured tenancy. Therefore, if the landlord did not comply with the requirements (a minimum term of six months and a notice given to the tenant before the tenant entered into the tenancy, making it clear that the new tenancy was to be an assured shorthold tenancy), then he created a full assured tenancy. One of the aims, however, of assured shorthold tenancies was to enable private individuals to grant tenancies without the need to consult a lawyer. The Housing Act 1996 now provides that for any tenancy entered into after 28 February 1997 the 'default' position is an assured shorthold tenancy. In other words, if the landlord does not specify that the tenancy will be an assured tenancy, it will be an assured shorthold tenancy. Possession of a property let on an assured shorthold tenancy can usually be recovered after two months.

It should be noted that, although the Housing Act 1988 is broadly favourable to the landlord, if he acts unlawfully and evicts his tenant without legal justification, he can be liable to pay compensation calculated on the basis of the value of the property without the tenant, less that value with the tenant in the property. This provision was presumably designed to remove from a landlord any profit that he made from an unlawful eviction. It can result in the landlord having to pay tens of thousands of pounds to a tenant. However, somewhat paradoxically, there is an argument that the value of a letting property (i.e. one divided into flats) is actually less with one tenant not in occupation since less rent is being received.

Business tenancies

The Landlord and Tenant Act 1954, Part II as amended by the Law of Property Act 1969, gives protection to business tenancies and is, therefore, important for people who are unable to purchase premises and who have to rent premises to carry on some form of equestrian business.

In order to come within the Act, there must be a tenancy. Property comprised in a tenancy must be or include premises occupied by the tenant and the tenant must occupy those premises for the purpose of a business carried on by himself. Although tenancy is given a wide meaning, it does not include (as was noted above), a tenancy at will created by agreement or by implication, nor does it include a licence, nor a tenancy of an agricultural holding. It is, therefore, important for a tenant to ensure that he has either a fixed term tenancy or a periodic tenancy if he wishes to carry on a business at the premises and wishes to be a protected tenant.

The requirement is that the premises should be occupied for the purposes of the business, which means that the premises may still be protected if they are used for the storage of hay, straw, horseboxes, etc., even though the actual riding or equestrian business is not carried on there. It is also open to a tenant to use the premises for two purposes, so the renting of a house and yard, where the tenant uses the yard to run a business, but lives in the house, does not necessarily preclude him from protection under the Act. It is a question of degree and clearly, when the business activity is not a significant use of the premises, it has been held that the premises were not occupied for the purpose of a business (*Cheryl Investment v Saldanha* [1979]).

The premises do not have to be buildings. It has been held that gallops were premises of which a racehorse trainer had a tenancy which was a business tenancy within the 1954 Act (*Bracey v Reed* [1962]).

113

The occupation itself must be genuine and it need not be by the tenant himself: it can be by his servants or agents. The occupation does not have to be continuous and it can be sufficient if the occupation is only for part of the year, if the business is seasonal (for instance pony trekking), provided the periods in occupation correspond with the seasonal nature of the business.

The protection given to a business tenant by Part II of the 1954 Act is not so extensive as that given to a residential tenant under the 1977 Rent Act. Put simply, and depending of course on the facts of the case, the tenant is entitled to call for a new tenancy to be fixed by the local County Court, if the landlord is unable to establish one of the seven grounds of objection set out in s.30 of the 1954 Act. These grounds include that the tenant has failed to fulfil his obligation to repair the premises, or has been persistently late in paying rent. If he establishes one of the grounds, the landlord will prevent the tenant from having a new tenancy, although, in certain circumstances, he is obliged to pay compensation to the tenant for the disruption which he, the tenant, has suffered to his business. However, the amount of compensation payable (which is calculated on the rateable value) is unlikely to be vast.

Agricultural tenancies

For a number of reasons, Parliament has decided to treat tenancies related to agriculture differently from other tenancies. Therefore, just as the Housing Act 1988 covers rented living accommodation and Part II of the Landlord and Tenant Act 1954 covers rented business premises, so both Acts have their counterparts in agriculture. The agriculture related Acts tend to be somewhat specialised and are not 'user-friendly' for the layman.

The Rent (Agriculture) Act 1976 covers living accommodation occupied by farm workers (i.e. tied cottages). It has its own list of words with specialised meaning and provides ways for obtaining possession which are not available in the rest of the dwelling house market. For example, if the Agricultural Dwelling-House Advisory Committee (ADHAC) considers that the property is required for an agricultural worker, there may be a duty on the local authority to rehouse the existing occupant.

Rented farmland used to be covered by the Agricultural Holdings Act 1986 (which was really a re-enactment of the Agricultural Holdings Act 1948 with various amendments). The thinking behind these Acts was to give tenant farmers protection against a landlord who, for example, might otherwise allow the tenant to invest a great deal of time, energy and money in the land and then, the week before harvest, oust the tenant and take the crops for himself. The 1986 Act, therefore, provided for lengthy periods of notice.It also gave the tenant farmer the right under certain circumstances to serve a counter notice. Serving the counter notice suspended the effect of any Notice to Quit unless and until the Agricultural Lands Tribunal gave its consent. However, most of these complex provisions have been consigned to history. The Agricultural Tenancies Act 1995 provides that any tenancy beginning on or after 1 September 1995 will not be governed by the 1986 Act. Obviously, agricultural holdings governed by the 1986 Act will exist for many years. However, since 1 September 1995, they have been replaced with farm business tenancies, which are more akin to business tenancies protected by Part II of the Landlord and Tenant Act 1954 than to the old agricultural holding.

Licences

Licences have been mentioned from time to time in this chapter and a definition should be provided. A person standing on land could be the freehold owner, the leasehold owner (i.e. a tenant), a licensee or a trespasser. The first two obviously have some interest in the land itself. The licensee has no interest in the land and thus less right than a tenant, but is not a trespasser; he has a personal permission (i.e. a licence) to be there, but no more. He may have paid for his licence (e.g. a visitor who pays to watch a three-day event) or he may not. Indeed, there are certain implied licences (e.g. the right of a caller to cross the owner's land to get to the front door).

A licence can be withdrawn whenever the giver of the licence decides to revoke it. How much notice he needs to give will depend upon the circumstances. A licence to view a particular event entitles the purchaser of the ticket to enter and (provided he behaves properly) to remain on the premises until the end of the event which he has paid to witness (see *Winter Garden Theatre (London) v Millennium Productions* [1948]). The giver of the licence will not normally be able to revoke it until the event is finished but, if the holder of the licence remained on the property after revocation, he would be a trespasser.

The advantage of a licence from the landlord's point of view is that it is not protected by the Housing Act 1988 (although some periodic licences now require a Notice to Quit to bring about a determination) or the Landlord and Tenant Act 1954, Part II. (However, some agricultural licences are protected by the Agricultural Holdings Act 1986.) Until recently landlords would frequently give people wishing to live in premises 'licence agreements' rather than 'tenancies' so as to be able to evict them if they wished. However, in *Street v Mountford* [1985] the House of Lords decided that it did not matter what the document called the agreement. Subject to certain exceptions, if it gave the occupier exclusive occupation of the premises for a period of time on the payment of money, it was a tenancy even if the document called it a licence. If, on the other hand, the landlord could enter the property whenever he wished as of right (not necessarily being a right reserved in a lease), for example to clean a room and change the bed linen of a lodger, that would be a licence. Accordingly, if a landlord now tries to evict somebody who only has a licence, the court will hear evidence and decide whether the document really created a licence or a tenancy.

Grazing agreements

The main equestrian application of the law relating to licences is in respect of grazing for a horse. Grass keep is sometimes sold by farmers or other landowners. This gives the purchaser the right to graze the land for a specified period, and for that period only, which is usually April to October. Sometimes a seasonal grazing licence is granted, whereby grass from land is taken during the grazing season in successive years. This type of licence is a licence to occupy land for grazing 'during some specified period of the year'. This comes within the proviso to s.2(1) of the Agricultural Holdings Act 1948 and cannot be a tenancy from year to year within s.2(1) (as amended by the Agricultural Holdings Act 1986) and is, therefore, not protected (*Watts v Yeend* [1987]).

Another common method of obtaining grazing is by contract of agistment, that is where a person, the agistor, takes another person's horse onto his land to graze for reward. This does not, however, create any interest in the land and does not have to be evidenced in writing. The agistor is not allowed to detain the horse, there being an implied term in the contract that the horse will be returned on demand. An agistor must take reasonable steps to exhibit proper care of the horses and protect them from dangers on the land, for instance barbed wire. In some circumstances, the agistor can be liable in negligence for injury caused as a result of his failure to take reasonable and proper care (*Smith v Cook* [1875]). If the owner of the horse is aware of the dangers, however, he is unlikely to have any valid claim. In general an agistor does not have any lien (or right to keep the horse in lieu of payment) upon the horse agisted, or grazing on his land.

Chapter 11 VETERINARY SURGEONS

'Veterinary Surgery' is the art and science of veterinary surgery and medicine. It includes:

a) the diagnosis of diseases in animals
b) the giving of advice based on the diagnosis
c) medical or surgical treatment of animals
d) the performance of surgical operations on animals.

The profession of veterinary surgery is regulated by the charters granted to the Royal College of Veterinary Surgeons and by the Veterinary Surgeons Act 1966 and other subordinate legislation.

The Royal College of Veterinary Surgeons

The Royal College of Veterinary Surgeons was incorporated in 1844 by Royal Charter. Other Charters have subsequently been granted and confirmed by statute. In 1967 a further Charter was granted which revoked all previous supplemental Charters and a substantial portion of the 1844 Charter. The 1967 Charter restates and consolidates the provisions of the previous Charters relating to the administration of the College, which are not covered by the Veterinary Surgeons Act 1966.

Composition

The Royal College of Veterinary Surgeons consists of fellows, members and honorary associates.

A fellow is a member who is elected to this position or has presented a thesis, passed an examination or made a meritorious contribution to learning.

Members of the College are those persons who are on the register of veterinary surgeons. In order to qualify to register a person must have either:

(i) obtained a university degree in veterinary surgery at a recognised university in the United Kingdom or the Republic of Ireland, or

(ii) passed examinations in veterinary surgery held by the Royal College of Surgeons at other universities in the United Kingdom, or

(iii) hold Commonwealth or foreign qualifications in veterinary surgery and have satisfied the council of the College by examination or otherwise, that he has the requisite knowledge and skill to fit him for practising veterinary surgery in the United Kingdom, or

(iv) hold recognised European qualifications in veterinary surgery.

Honorary associates are persons elected to this position by the council of the College, usually because they are of special eminence or have given special service to veterinary science or the veterinary profession.

There is a supplementary veterinary register which contains the names of 'veterinary practitioners', that is:

1. Persons registered in this register immediately before the commencement of the Veterinary Surgeons Act 1966.

2. Persons who were registered at some previous time, but were not registered immediately before the commencement of the 1966 Act, but whose names have been restored to the register on the direction of the disciplinary committee of the College.
3. Persons, who for a total of not less than seven out of the preceding ten years immediately preceding 2 December 1965 held a licence under the provisions of the Veterinary Surgeons Act 1948, permitting the licensing of employees of certain societies and institutions providing free treatment for animals.

A person who is not a registered veterinary surgeon or a registered veterinary practitioner and who holds himself out as practising or as being prepared to practise veterinary surgery commits an offence, which is punishable on both summary conviction and on indictment to a fine.

Government

The government of the College is vested in a council. This consists of thirty elected members and such additional persons as may be elected or appointed in accordance with any agreement between the British Government and the Government of the Irish Republic.

This council undertakes the management of the College. It is able to make certain rules and regulations, but these will not take effect unless approved by order of the Privy Council. An important function is the supervision of the courses of study and examinations. The council is controlled overall by the Privy Council, which may direct the College to discharge its functions under the Veterinary Surgeons Act 1966.

Disciplinary procedures

The council has a disciplinary committee which may exercise its powers if:

(i) a registered veterinary surgeon or registered veterinary practitioner is convicted in the United Kingdom or elsewhere of a criminal offence, which in the committee's opinion renders him unfit to practise veterinary surgery, or
(ii) any such person is judged by the committee to have been guilty

of disgraceful conduct* in any professional respect, or

(iii) the committee is satisfied that the name of such person has been fraudulently entered in the register, either of veterinary surgeons or the supplemental register.

*Disgraceful conduct will be a matter of fact but in *Plenderleith v Royal College of Veterinary Surgeons* [1996] 1WLR 224 it was held that unlawful conduct may not necessarily amount to disgraceful conduct in special cases.

The committee has the power, in these circumstances, to direct that the person's name be removed from the appropriate register or that his registration be suspended. Suspension will not, however, be considered where there is a fraudulent entry. Notice of any direction made by the committee must be served upon the person concerned.

There is a 'preliminary investigation committee' set up by the council. The committee consists of the president and vice-president of the College and three members of the council, elected by the council. This committee is under a duty to conduct a preliminary investigation into every disciplinary case and decide whether the case should be referred to the disciplinary committee.

The disciplinary committee consists of a chairman and eleven other members, all of whom are elected. They must be members of the council, with not less than six of them being elected members and at least one being appointed to the council by the Privy Council.

A member of the preliminary investigation committee in respect of a particular case cannot sit on the disciplinary committee for the same case.

It is the duty of the disciplinary committee to consider and determine any disciplinary case referred to it by the preliminary investigation committee and any case for the restoration of a name to the register or the removal of a suspension of registration.

The rules of the procedure to be followed and the rules of evidence to be observed are made by the council of the Royal College. These rules do not come into force until approved by order of the Privy Council.

Under the Veterinary Surgeons Act 1966, in all proceedings there must be an assessor to the committee to advise the committee on questions of law which arise. The assessor must have a ten-year general qualification. The assessor must be present at all proceedings before the disciplinary committee in respect of the removal from or restoration to the register of a person's name. He must advise the committee on points of law and the admission of evidence. He must inform the committee of any irregularities which may arise and of any possibilities of a mistake of law being made, save for his own advice.

The assessor's advice must be given in the presence of every party, or their representatives. Where a question is put to the assessor during the private deliberations of the committee and it is felt that it would be prejudicial to the discharge of their duties to tender this advice in public, it may be tendered in the parties' absence, but they must be informed of the question put to the assessor and the advice tendered. Such advice should be put in writing and a copy made available to the parties.

Where the committee does not accept the assessor's advice, a record must be made of the question referred, of the advice given, and of the refusal to accept it. Reasons for the refusal should be recorded and a copy must be given to the parties or their representatives.

Where the case relates to conduct or to a conviction, once the case has been referred to the disciplinary committee, the registrar must serve on the respondent a notice of inquiry. This notice must specify the matters alleged against him in the form of a charge or charges. This must also set out the day, time and place that the committee will hold an inquiry; a copy of the rules should also be sent. The same procedure applies when a case is referred to the committee by the preliminary investigation committee. An inquiry cannot be held unless a notice of inquiry has been served on the respondent.

Any party to an inquiry relating to conduct or to a conviction is entitled, upon application and payment of the proper charges, to copies of any statutory declaration, explanation, answer, admission or other statement or communication sent to the Royal College by any party to the inquiry. A party to an inquiry is entitled to legal representation, whether by counsel or solicitor.

Generally, all proceedings before the disciplinary committee must take place in the presence of all the parties to the proceedings and must be held in public. In certain circumstances, the committee may deliberate *in camera* with the public excluded. The announcement of the determination of the committee must be given in public.

The first act in the disciplinary proceedings is the reading of the charge in the presence of the respondent. The respondent can object to the charge or any part of it on a point of law. The solicitor nominated by the Royal College may answer any objection and the respondent has the right of final reply.

Where the case concerns an allegation of a criminal offence making him unfit to practise veterinary surgery, and the respondent appears, then the registrar will ask the respondent if he admits the conviction. Where the respondent does not admit the conviction or does not appear, then the registrar will adduce evidence of the conviction. Similarly, where the case is one of misconduct, then the registrar will ask the respondent, if he appears, whether he admits the charges: again if he does not, or does not appear, the solicitor will adduce evidence of the facts not admitted.

The respondent has the right to address the committee on the charges themselves and may also adduce evidence as to the nature and circumstances of the offence, to show that he is not unfit, by reason of the offences, to practise veterinary surgery. Where such evidence is adduced, the solicitor may adduce evidence in rebuttal.

In a case relating to conduct the respondent can, at the end of the case against him, make a submission of no case to answer, in other words that there is insufficient evidence that would enable the committee to find the facts alleged against him proved. The respondent may also submit that the facts alleged against him do not amount to disgraceful conduct in any professional respect. Both submissions may be made. The solicitor may answer the submission and the respondent has the right to a final reply.

Once the submissions have been made, the committee must consider the submission and make a ruling; such ruling must be announced by the chairman in appropriate terms.

Where the submission is not upheld, or a submission is not made, the respondent may adduce evidence in answer to the charges and the evidence thereof. The respondent has the right to address the committee. The solicitor may call evidence in rebuttal, but the respondent has a right of reply in respect of that rebuttal evidence. The solicitor can address the committee in reply to the respondent's case in the following circumstances:

(i) if oral evidence is given on the respondent's behalf, other than that of the respondent himself (save where the evidence is evidence of character); or

(ii) with the leave of the committee, where no such evidence has been given; or

(iii) if the respondent has made a submission on a point of law, save that the solicitor's right to reply is limited to that submission.

Where the solicitor has a right to address the committee, the respondent has a final right of reply.

It is open to the committee to receive oral, documentary or other evidence of any fact which appears relevant to the case before it. However, where the form in which the evidence is tendered would not be admissible in criminal proceedings in an English court, the committee may not receive evidence of it, unless after consultation with the legal assessor the committee is satisfied that the interests of justice dictate that the evidence should be admitted. The committee is entitled to take into account the difficulty and expense of obtaining evidence which would be admissible. The committee may call its own witnesses, and questions may be put to any witness by the committee, with leave of the chairman, through the chairman or by the legal assessor.

The proceedings must be recorded by a shorthand writer and any party must be supplied with a copy of the transcript of the proceedings in 'open court'. An appropriate fee will have to be paid.

When the proceedings are finished the committee has to consider in cases relating to conviction:

a) whether the facts alleged have been proved

b) whether the respondent has been convicted of an offence which, in the committee's opinion, renders him unfit to practise veterinary surgery.

The chairman, upon the committee coming to a decision, must announce the findings.

In conduct cases, the committee must consider whether the facts alleged in the charge or charges have been proved to its satisfaction. Again, after deliberation the findings must be announced.

Where the committee finds the facts alleged proved, or there has been a finding against the respondent, the chairman must then invite the solicitor to address the committee on the respondent's character and previous history. He may adduce evidence of this. The respondent has a right to address the committee by way of mitigation.

The committee then considers its judgment, which it can deliver immediately or postpone to another day. A postponement cannot last more than two years. Once judgment is passed, the committee must consider whether the name of the respondent should be removed from the register or suspended, or whether a warning as to future conduct will be sufficient.

Where the disciplinary committee is deciding whether an entry in the register is fraudulent, the solicitor must send the respondent a notice of inquiry. A copy of the notice must be sent to each party to the case. The procedure followed is similar to that already described. If it is determined that it is a fraudulent entry, then the entry must be removed from the register.

Once the name of a person is removed from the register or suspended from the register, in pursuance of a direction by the committee, the name cannot be entered on the register again until an application is made to the committee for restoration and the committee so directs. Such an application cannot be made within ten months of the date of the removal or suspension or a previous application.

There is a right of appeal against the committee's decision. This lies to the Privy Council and must be made within twenty-eight days of the service of the notice of direction from the committee. Where an appeal is brought the direction does not take place until such time as the appeal may be heard and dismissed.

If an appeal is withdrawn the direction takes effect on that withdrawal.

Professional Standards

When a veterinary surgeon is asked provide a service for the client he is entering into a contract. If something goes wrong with this service, it is, however, more likely in practice that any claim will be in negligence rather than under the laws of contract.

Veterinary surgeons and practitioners are expected to exercise the ordinary standard of skill, which is to be expected of a member of the veterinary profession. If their treatment of an animal falls below that standard, they are likely to be sued in negligence. In addition, if a veterinary surgeon hands over a case to his assistant who is negligent, it was held in *Chute Farms Ltd v Curtis* (1961), that the veterinary surgeon will be vicariously liable for the assistant's negligence. When examining a horse for a purchaser, a veterinary surgeon is expected to spot any defect that a prudent and careful veterinary surgeon would have spotted. A failure to do so may give rise to a claim in negligence.

A veterinary surgeon is also responsible for the drugs he supplies in that there is an implied warranty that the substance given is reasonably fit for the purpose for which it is required, i.e. for administering to animals. See *Dodd and Dodd v Wilson and McWilliam* [1946] 2 All ER 691.

(The issues mentioned in this section have also been covered in Chapter 2 Negligence, and Chapter 4 Buying and Selling.)

Chapter 12 BETTING AND GAMING ON HORSES

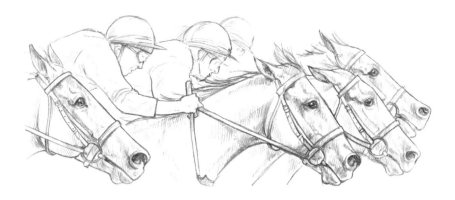

In line with the subject matter of this book, this chapter is concerned primarily with betting on horses. Whilst the term gaming is often confused with betting, horseracing, as a sport, is specifically excluded from the statutory definition of 'gaming' (section 52(1) Gaming Act 1968). Incidentally, it should be stated at this juncture that the winning of trophies and prize money by the owners of racehorses is not illegal, albeit a form of gaming, because of the exclusion of 'any athletic game or sport' from the definition of 'gaming' set out in section 51 of the Gaming Act 1968.

The activities of betting and gaming are not in themselves illegal. They are amongst mankind's oldest vices, and any attempt to prevent such activities would be futile. Instead, UK governments have sought to regulate and control betting and gaming so as to protect the vulnerable and to minimise the involvement of criminals.

Despite the advent of betting on a variety of sports, betting on horseracing is still the most popular form, and an important function of both the British Horseracing Board (BHB) and the Jockey

Club has been to maintain the integrity of horseracing as a betting medium. The simple reason for this is that current legislation provides for a levy on betting on horseracing to be paid to the BHB under the control of the Horserace Betting Levy Board.

That situation is under threat from the establishment of offshore bookmaking enterprises, with which bets placed via the internet avoid payment of both betting duty (tax) and the betting levy. As an industry, horseracing is keen to establish new ways of funding through broadcasting rights, and the government is having to grapple with the problems caused by increasing access to on-line, offshore betting facilities.

As stated, betting as an activity is quite legal. Therefore, two people, disagreeing as to which horse might win a race can, quite legally, bet with each other so that one wins and the other loses. Betting of this kind was commonly known as a wager. The term 'betting' is not defined in statute. In the famous case of *Carlill v Carbolic Smoke Ball Co* (1892) 2 QB 484, Hawkins J made this statement regarding a wagering contract: '... if either of the parties can win but cannot lose or may lose but cannot win, it is not a wagering contract'. In other words, there has to be a situation where both parties to the wager can either win or lose.

The importance of this definition lies in the continuing legal state of affairs that wagering contracts are not enforceable by virtue of The Gaming Act 1845. So it is that bookmakers cannot enforce bad debts. Most betting, however, is in the form of cash or pre-payment betting so that the question of enforcement by the bookmaker rarely exists.

Besides wagering, the other common form of 'betting' is pool betting. In this instance the organiser of the 'pool' – usually known as the 'promoter' – accepts bets from members of the public, places the monies into a pool, removes his profits, expenses and tax and divides the residue amongst the winners. A would-be pools promoter has to register with the local authority as such and is subject to regular audits.

In horseracing the most common form of pool betting is with 'the Tote' (the Horseracing Totalisator Board). The Tote has a monopoly of pool betting in relation to organised horseracing

(Section 14 Betting Gaming and Lotteries Act 1963). If, for example, the local hunt wishes to operate a tote at its point-to-point meeting, it must first obtain the authorisation of the Tote.

Bookmaking

The Betting Gaming and Lotteries Act 1963 prohibits commercial betting on the street, in public places and in places to which the public has access. It does so by making illegal the activity of bookmaking except in clearly defined and controlled circumstances.

Commercial operators are either bookmakers or pools promoters. 'Bookmakers' are defined under section 55 of The Betting Gaming and Lotteries Act 1963 as: '... any person other than the Totalisator Board who:

a) whether on his own account or as a servant or agent to any other person, carries on, whether occasionally or regularly, the business of receiving or negotiating bets or conducting pool betting operations; or

b) by way of business in any manner holds himself out or permits himself to be held out, as a person who receives or negotiates bets or conducts such operations.'

This very wide trawl was intended to cover all illegal street and factory betting operations, which existed prior to the introduction of this legislation in 1960.

Bookmaker's permit

In order to be able to operate legally, either on a racecourse ('on-course') or in a betting shop or by telephone (off-course'), a bookmaker has to hold a bookmaker's permit. To act as a bookmaker without a permit is a criminal offence which carries an unlimited fine and up to one year's imprisonment.

An application for a bookmaker's permit must be made to the Betting Licensing Committee (a committee of local justices), in the area in which the bookmaker resides or has his principal office. A limited company can hold a bookmaker's permit. The application can be made at any time but will be dealt with on one of the days fixed by the committee for the conduct of its business each year.

There is a prescribed form for application and the procedures set out in Schedule 1 to the 1963 Betting Gaming and Lotteries Act demand strict compliance. Failure to give proper notices, to serve all required parties (e.g. police and Customs and Excise), or to advertise, will result in a refused application. Personal references are required as to the fitness of the applicant to hold a licence, and the police will carry out checks.

Betting office licence

In order to provide bookmaking services to members of the public in the high street a bookmaker needs a betting office licence for the premises concerned. Such licences are granted by the same committee of local justices as grant permits, and they have to be satisfied as to the suitability of the premises, not only as to their construction and layout but also as to their location. It is unlikely, therefore, that a betting office licence would be granted for premises next to a school. The justices also have a discretion to refuse to grant a betting office licence if they are of the view that there are sufficient in a locality to meet an existing demand. A betting office licence costs £125 and £25 on renewal.

Duration and renewal of permit and licence

Both bookmaker's permits and betting office licences last for three years. There are detailed provisions as to renewal, which give to the authorities and members of the public the right to object. In addition, the committee has power to cancel a permit or a licence if the provisions of the Act have been broken.

There are rights of appeal against the refusal to grant or renew a bookmaker's permit or betting office licence, or against cancellation. The Crown Court hears any such appeal and its decision is final. Again, the provisions are set out in detail in the schedules to the 1963 Act.

There is also a rarely used provision for people acting on behalf of a bookmaker to hold what is known as a betting agency permit. Such a permit affords the same rights as the full bookmaker's permits, but because the procedures to be followed are exactly the same and the fees to be paid are exactly the same (£160 on grant – £20 on renewal) there seems little point in applying for a betting agency permit.

Approved horse racecourses and tracks

Apart from licensed offices, the other exception to prohibition on commercial betting in public places is for approved racecourses and tracks. Approval for a racecourse is given by the Horserace Betting Levy Board. Wherever officially approved racing takes place on an approved racecourse, betting with bookmakers is allowed.

On such racecourses will be found bookmakers, who have 'pitches' for which they will have paid. They either display boards indicating the prices offered or shout the odds from their places 'on the rails', usually between the general enclosure (known as 'Tattersalls') and the members' enclosure, in which will be found many of their credit clients. Bookmakers have to pay a daily admission fee, which goes to the racecourse, but betting with bookmakers on the racecourse is exempt from betting duty (tax). Racecourses also provide tote facilities (run by the Tote) and betting offices.

Licensed tracks

'Licensed tracks' are normally dog or greyhound racecourses, but the term can include any sports ground other than a horse racecourse. The local authority is responsible for the grant of licences. The existence of a track betting licence enables bookmaking to take place and, in the case of a greyhound track, for there to be a tote or pool betting operation.

Provisions for non-licensed tracks

In addition, provision is made for non-licensed tracks or racecourses to operate for not more than seven days in any year. This allows bookmaking to take place on an occasional basis at point-to-points, county shows and cricket grounds used perhaps once or twice a year. There is no prohibition on pool betting in such places but, as has been pointed out, the Tote monopoly means that pool betting is not available at horseracing events without prior approval. The Tote guards this monopoly jealously.

Charitable Events

The Gaming Act 1968 and the Lotteries and Amusements Act 1976 contain exemptions for charitable events. For example, section 41 of the Gaming Act 1968 allows equal chance gaming for limited prizes and small stakes to take place at 'an entertainment promoted otherwise than for the purposes of private gain'. The definition of private gain is wide enough to prevent commercial profit being made from any gaming activity.

Of more use to fund raisers, however, is the exemption given by section 15 of the Lotteries and Amusements Act 1976 which, taken together with section 1 of the Gaming Act 1968, enables any form of gaming or lottery to take place provided that certain conditions are met. These are:

a) that the whole proceeds of the entertainment, after deducting the legitimate expenses of the entertainment, must be devoted to purposes other than private gain; and

b) the facilities for winning prizes at amusements (by gaming or lottery) taken either individually or together must not be the only, or only substantial, inducement to persons to attend the entertainment.

The same kind of exemption does not apply to betting or pool betting. This means that, unless bookmakers can be persuaded to offer their services free of charge and donate their profits, then on a racecourse, licensed track or at a legal unlicensed event, betting activities are not appropriate for a fund-raising event. The only exception is the operation of a tote (with authorisation from the Tote) on an unlicensed track at, for example, a point-to-point. This distinction is often overlooked when race nights are organised by charitable concerns. Most race nights include forms of pool betting: some provide betting similar to that with bookmakers. It is probable that, despite the charitable intentions of the organisers, both activities are, strictly speaking, illegal.

Chapter 13 RULES AND DISCIPLINARY PROCEDURES OF EQUESTRIAN BODIES

Almost all disciplines of the equestrian sporting world in the UK used to come under the umbrella of the British Horse Society, horseracing being a notable exception. That situation has changed, and there are now individual bodies governing the various disciplines. This means that each discipline produces its own rule book and undertakes any disciplinary procedures which may be necessary. Both the British Show Jumping Association (BSJA) and British Eventing (formerly the British Horse Trials Association) are members of the British Equestrian Federation (BEF) and any appeal in disciplinary matters is to that body. I have not included the Endurance Societies' rules in this section as I understand that it is proposed to amalgamate the Societies, and no doubt new rules will be prepared as a consequence. It should also be borne in mind that individual breed societies have their own rules, and these will have to be adhered to.

Each individual body produces its own rule book: these are published annually and may contain amendments to the previous year's rules. It is prudent, therefore, to ensure that, if competing in a particular discipline, one is aware of the current rules. This chapter deals with the rules (current at the time of writing) relating to conduct of members, disciplinary procedures where there are breaches of the rules, and appeal procedures. Detailed rules for competitions will be found in the relevant rule book.

Although this chapter is fundamentally concerned with the self-contained rules of individual bodies and associations, there is one piece of statutory legislation that has implications for the drafting of such rules. The Horses (Free Access to Competitions) Regulations 1992 provide that the rules of any equestrian competition, including horseracing, showjumping, eventing, dressage, events reserved for horse drawn vehicles and showing classes, must not discriminate between horses which are registered or originate in the UK and horses which are registered or originate in another member state of the European Union. These regulations do not apply to competitions reserved for the purpose of permitting the improvement of the breed, regional competitions with a view to selecting horses, or historic or traditional events.

The Jockey Club

Horseracing has long had its own rules and these are set out in the Orders and Instructions of the British Horse Racing Board and the Rules of Racing and Instructions of the Jockey Club. The Jockey Club rules are comprehensive and cover all aspects of racing. There are orders, rules and instructions, all of which have to be adhered to. I do not propose to set these out in full, since they these are contained in the rule book published annually. However, I will deal with the rules, orders and instructions insofar as they relate to discipline, with particular emphasis on the appeal procedure.

It is the stewards of the Jockey Club who deal with matters of breaches of the rules and discipline. The stewards at a particular race meeting (of whom there must be at least four, and more if there are more than nine races), will determine all questions arising with reference to that race meeting, and will report such matters to the stewards of the Jockey Club. In particular, under rule 1A 2, when any person subject to the rules of racing has, in the opinion of the stewards of the Jockey Club:

(i)   committed any breach thereof, or

(ii) is guilty of an offence, or

(iii) is otherwise liable to a penalty under the Rules of Racing

the stewards of the Jockey Club have the power at their discretion to impose any one or more of these penalties:

a) A fine not exceeding £35,000

b) Declare him a disqualified person.

There are, however, some rules where the penalties for the breach are set out. In those circumstances the penalty imposed by the rule must be given.

Where there has been an enquiry and the stewards of the Jockey Club have found that a person has breached the rules of riding, they have various discretionary powers.

Where a rider breaches:

a) Sub rules 151(ii), (iii)* which relate to the rider ensuring that the horse has every opportunity of winning and the duty of the trainer to ensure that adequate instructions are given and that no owner or trainer shall give any instruction, which if followed could prevent a horse from winning or obtaining the best possible placing.

b) Sub rules 152 (iii), (iv), (v) which relate to running the wrong side of a running rail or marker, missing a fence or hurdle, disregarding of markers and failing to pull up or correct the error.

c) Sub rule 153(iii) which relates to intentional interference, reckless, irresponsible, careless or improper riding at *any* time on the racecourse including before or after any race.

d) Sub rule 160(I) which states that the riders of the first, second and third horses must ride their horses to the appointed place and all riders must present themselves for weighing. Riders must also report any reason for failing to complete the course.

Then the stewards of the Jockey Club can in their discretion:
a) suspend the rider from riding in a particular race or races and\or
b) suspend the rider from any race on a particular day or days and\or
c) suspend the rider from riding in any race for such period or periods as they think fit or
d) caution the rider as to future conduct in races.

*Where both a rider and trainer are found to have committed a breach of sub rule 151 then the stewards of the Jockey Club have the power to suspend the horse from running in such race or races and for such period of time as they think fit.

The stewards of the Jockey Club also have the power to withdraw or suspend the licence or permit of any person who is in breach of the rules.

There is a right of appeal against any decision of the stewards. This appeal lies to the stewards of the Jockey Club. The procedure for appeal is as follows:

1. The appellant shall lodge a Notice of Appeal with the Jockey Club office within seven days. The exception to this is the breach of sub-rules within sub-rule 153(iv)(a) or sub-rule 151(iii) in which case the appeal must be lodged with forty-eight hours of the decision being announced. Where Saturday, Sunday, Bank Holiday, Good Friday or Christmas Day intervenes it must be lodged on the first day thereafter that the Jockey Club is open for business.
2. A deposit of £350 must be made at the same time as the Notice of Appeal.
3. Where the appeal concerns a suspension under rule 17 then the suspension will not take effect pending the hearing.
4. The Notice of Appeal must be signed by the appellant, his authorised agent or his solicitor.

5. The Notice of Appeal must state the grounds of appeal in general terms.

6. Where the appeal is from the imposition of a fine of £250 or less the Notice of Appeal should state whether the appellant wishes to have:

   a) a personal hearing

   b) the appeal to be decided by submission of written evidence.

7. Where there is an appeal by submission of written evidence the appellant must within seven days of lodging the Notice of Appeal submit to the registry office (this being at present at the Jockey Club) such written evidence and representations as he may wish to make.

8. The stewards of the Jockey Club may request the stewards who made the original decision to submit written evidence. [It is not clear whether the appellant has the opportunity to see these submissions.]

9. The stewards of the Jockey Club can require further information to enable them to consider the appeal and they can direct to this end that a written summary of evidence be prepared by a person designated by them.

10. This written summary must be signed by the appellant, presumably to indicate that he agrees the evidence.

11. If the appellant does not sign the written summary of evidence then the stewards will treat the appeal as one where the appellant has required a personal hearing.

12. The appeal is considered by the stewards of the Jockey Club. Where the appeal is to be dealt with in the appellant's absence, the stewards will communicate the decision in writing to the appellant before it is published in the *Racing Calendar*.

The stewards of the Jockey Club may confirm or reverse or otherwise vary the decision of the racecourse stewards and may also exercise any of the stewards' powers under rule 2.

Where an appeal against a suspension under rule 153(iv) is dismissed, any suspension imposed will commence either on the date in accordance with the instruction H16 or, if the appeal has not been

concluded by that date, the suspension will start on the day following that on which a decision on the appeal is given.

Where an appeal against a suspension under rule 17 is dismissed, any suspension imposed shall commence on the day following that upon which the decision on the appeal is given unless
the stewards of the Jockey Club direct otherwise.

No appeal against a rule 17 suspension may be withdrawn without the consent of the stewards of the Jockey Club who may, in their
discretion, impose conditions in relation to the suspension, including any dates for the suspension, any orders as to costs and forfeiture of the deposit.

So far as costs generally are concerned, under rule 2(vi)(b) the
stewards of the Jockey Club shall have the power to order the appellant to pay reasonable costs and expenses relating to the appeal. This
power is discretionary, in other words it is a decision of the stewards
of the Jockey Club. They also have a similar discretion to order such
reasonable compensation for any outlay in connection with the
appeal as they may decide.

The British Show Jumping Association

The British Show Jumping Association is another body that has been
self-governing. Its rules are set out in the rules and year-book, which
is sent to members automatically. The rules themselves cover:
Organisation of the BSJA
Administration
Membership
Registration of Horses and Ponies
Grading

The actual running of competitions is fully covered under Jumping
and Judging. There are rules for special competitions and qualifying
competitions.

Conduct and discipline are covered under rules 81–99.

It is important to appreciate that, by completing a membership
application form, a person has agreed to be bound by the

Memorandum and Articles of Association and all rules, regulations and by-laws made thereunder and has agreed that the decisions of the executive board, stewards and other competent authorities of the Association given in accordance with the rules shall be binding.

Rule 82, sub-rules 1–21 covers the conduct of members of the BSJA, dealing both with behaviour of the member towards the public and towards their horse.

Rule 82.14 is a rule to note as it prohibits members from competing, or officiating save in certain capacities, as owners or riders at an unaffiliated show where a prize is more than £10. (See also rules 72.2 and 71.3.)

The Executive Board of the BSJA appoints stewards who consider complaints of misconduct and are also able to impose appropriate penalties. The penalties which the stewards can impose are:

a) That the member be reprimanded and cautioned as to future conduct.

b) That the member may be suspended from all or any privileges of membership for a period not exceeding five years.

c) That any horse or pony belonging to or ridden by the member at the time of the misconduct may be disbarred or disqualified from certain competitions for a period not exceeding twelve months.

d) That a fine be paid.

Complaints of misconduct by a member must be made in writing to the Chief Executive, save where the complaint arises in Scotland, in which case the procedure is different. (See rule 88).

The Chief Executive has the power to impose penalties on members where there have been minor infringements of the rules 22 to 79 inclusive. This also applies to rules 82.14, 82.15 and 82.16 subject to the right of any member to have the matter referred to the stewards or the Scottish Branch stewards.

Where it is not a matter to be dealt with by the Chief Executive, notice will be sent to the member giving the time and place of the stewards' meeting at least three weeks prior to the meeting. Details will also be given of the nature of the complaint and the names of any witnesses.

A member may in these circumstances appear in person at the stewards' meeting and may give oral or written evidence. The member may also call and examine witnesses or submit written evidence and statements to be considered in his absence. The stewards may reach a decision and impose a penalty in the member's absence if he fails to appear (rule 86.1).

No member is entitled to be represented by a third party and this presumably includes legal representation. Juniors or junior associate members must always be accompanied by the responsible adult (see rule 33.4) and an associate member may be accompanied by an adult member of their immediate family (rule 86.20).

Where a member is convicted in a British court of law of any membership-related equestrian offence, for instance cruelty to animals, he may be immediately suspended from all rights or privileges of membership pending a full investigation by the stewards at any enquiry under rule 83.

Where incidents complained of arise in Scotland, complaint should be made in writing to the Administrator of the Scottish Branch. There is then a preliminary investigation by the standing committee of the Scottish Branch. If it is considered that a prima facie case of misconduct exists, they will refer it to the Scottish Branch stewards. The stewards may convene a meeting to deal with the matter unless it is felt that the misconduct is such that it could be dealt with summarily under rule 91, in which case the matter will be referred to the Chief Executive.

The Scottish Branch stewards can also impose penalties:
a) A caution or reprimand as to future conduct.
b) Suspension from rights or privileges of membership for up to twelve months.
c) Debarring of a horse or pony from competing in certain competitions for up to twelve months.
d) A fine not exceeding £500.

The Scottish Branch stewards may at any time refer a matter to the Chief Executive if they consider the misconduct is so serious that it should be considered by the stewards of the Association.

Within seven days of any decision by the appropriate body, both the complainant and the accused should be notified in writing of the findings and any penalties imposed. These findings and penalties are final and binding on all parties under rule 90.2. Nonetheless, there is a right of appeal to the British Equestrian Federation's appeal committee within twenty-eight days of the stewards' decision. Any appeal will be subject to the British Equestrian Federation's Terms of Reference. The parties to the appeal will be notified in writing at least twenty-one days before the hearing as to the time, date and place of the hearing, and will also receive a written statement which sets out the substance of the appeal or referral. Any party is entitled to be represented, or to appear in person and give oral evidence.

British Eventing (Formerly BHTA)

The rules of British Eventing are to be found in their rule book published annually. All members have to accept the rules and will be bound by them, and making an entry for any horse trial constitutes acceptance of the rules and agreement to be bound by them.

Their rules have a restriction similar to that of the BSJA, in that affiliated horses and riders may not compete in unaffiliated horse trials where the total value of the prizes offered exceeds £75 per section. This does not apply to Affiliated Riding Clubs or Pony Club horse trials.

Disciplinary matters are set out under rule 3. The general issue for discipline is that of 'disgraceful conduct'. This applies to any member of British Eventing and any person participating in any way at a horse trial to which these rules apply, including FEI events.

The three categories of disgraceful conduct are:
1. Behaving with incivility or contempt towards an official.
2. Acting in a manner which is prejudicial to the integrity, proper conduct or good reputation of horse trials or British Eventing. [It is presumably under this category that most matters are dealt with, i.e. breaches of specific rules and in particular excessive use of the whip and use of banned substances.]
3. Aiding or abetting the commission of any breach of these rules.

The use of the whip, spurs and bit are important matters and how each are to be used is specifically set out in Annexe 5 of the rules. Breaches concerning these items will only be dealt with by way of a caution in very minor cases or if the British Eventing steward is not completely satisfied with the evidence. (This raises an interesting point. Does this mean that if the steward is not satisfied that there has been improper use that he will caution the alleged offender? As an aside, this is quite contrary to the police method of cautioning, which is on the basis of the offender admitting the offence!) The usual penalty for excessive use of the whip, spurs or bit will be disqualification from the event together with a fine in the range of £75–£100. If the horse has already been eliminated, which is quite possible, the rider may also be disqualified from riding any other horse at the event and will still be subject to the fine.

Matters of discipline are dealt with initially by the disciplinary steward who will be the British Eventing steward. The disciplinary steward is empowered, if in his opinion there has been a breach of the rules, to caution the person and impose all or any of these penalties:
A reprimand.
Disqualification of the horse from that event.
Disqualification of the rider from that event.
A fine of up to £100.

The disciplinary steward may, as an alternative to the above, or in addition to any disqualification, refer the matter to the disciplinary committee. The chairman of the disciplinary committee is appointed by the board and the committee shall consist of three members. The committee will determine matters referred to it and any appeals permitted under the rules, in particular, against a fine or disqualification. Where it gives a decision on an appeal that decision shall be final.

Any appeal to the disciplinary committee must be made in writing and must be received, together with a fee of £40, by the Director of Horse Trials within ten days of the date of the decision that is the subject of the appeal.

If a disciplinary steward is unable to conclude a disciplinary matter at an official horse trial, or immediately afterwards, he may within seven days of the end of the event refer the matter to the Director of Horse Trials. When a matter has been referred to the Director of Horse Trials and it seems to him that a person may have been in breach of the rules, he has the power to impose the same penalties as a disciplinary steward or to refer the matter to the disciplinary committee.

Any matter which is referred to the disciplinary committee will be determined by the committee in accordance with the rules of natural justice. There is no specific mention in the rules one way or the other, but this presumably means that the person concerned has the right to be represented, if they so wish.

If the disciplinary committee decides that there has been a breach of the rules, it may decide to take no further action, or it may impose any or all of the following penalties.

1. A reprimand.
2. Disqualification of the horse and /or rider from any horse trials, to which the rules apply, in which horse or rider have taken part.
3. Suspension of horse and /or rider or trainer or any other person participating in any horse trial to which these rules apply, for a period not exceeding two years from the date of the committee's decision, or from the date of the first horse trial in the spring or autumn season following the date of the committee's decision.
4. A fine not exceeding £500.
5. Suspension from membership of British Eventing for a period not exceeding two years.

The committee may allow or dismiss an appeal. If any appeal is dismissed the committee may either confirm the penalty or may reduce or increase it. Where an appeal is allowed, any fine will be refunded and any disqualification removed. Removal of disqualification will not alter any placings of the horses in the competition but the committee may award such points to the disqualified horse as it deems fit and British Eventing may be directed to pay such prize money as the committee deems appropriate.

The committee has an absolute discretion to order any party to an appeal to pay all or part of any costs incurred by the other party (rule 3.c(viii)).

As is the case with the BSJA, a person who is found by the committee to have been in breach of the rules will have the right to appeal to the disciplinary committee of the British Equestrian Federation. The BEF may, at any hearing, reduce, confirm or increase any penalty or suspension previously imposed.

The appeal is subject to a formal procedure namely:

1. Notice of an appeal, together with a fee of £100, must be given to the Director of Horse Trials within fourteen days of the decision of the disciplinary committee.

2. The notice of appeal shall clearly state whether the appeal is against the finding of the breach of the rules, or the penalty, or both.

Any suspension shall not be put into force until such time as the appeal has been heard and a decision made by the BEF disciplinary committee.

Where an appeal against suspension is withdrawn by the appellant prior to the appeal being determined by the BEF disciplinary committee, any prize money, points or qualification obtained by the appellant between lodging the appeal and withdrawing it shall be forfeited and cancelled. This is an interesting rule and is, no doubt, designed to prevent appeals which have no merit.

Where an appeal against a suspension is withdrawn, the period of suspension will run either from the date of the withdrawal or the first day of March next, at the discretion of the disciplinary committee.

Where an appeal against a fine is successful the fine will be refunded.

The disciplinary committee of the BEF has an absolute discretion to order any party to an appeal to pay the costs incurred by the other party or by the BEF. In general the party bringing the appeal shall be responsible for the whole of the cost of the appeal, including those costs incurred by the BEF and British Eventing.

Where fines or costs are imposed the person on whom they are imposed shall not participate in any official horse trials to which these rules apply until such time as the whole of the fines or costs are paid to British Eventing.

British Dressage

In the British Dressage rule book, conduct and discipline are covered by rules 97–115. As with the BSJA, every member of British Dressage has, by the completion of the membership form, agreed to be bound by the rules of British Dressage (rule 97.1).

British Dressage has a rule similar to those of the BSJA and British Eventing, in that members of British Dressage are not permitted to take part in unaffiliated competitions where any prize exceeds £10 for dressage or £15 for dressage with jumping, or where a prize in kind exceeds those values, unless there is special permission from British Dressage for the organiser of the competition to offer such prizes.

Rule 109 allows for the appointment of disciplinary stewards at competitions and a disciplinary steward who considers that there is a breach of the rules may:

a) reprimand
b) disqualify the horse and /or rider
c) suspend the horse and/or rider from any class at the competition.

The disciplinary steward may, within fourteen days of the end of the event, refer the matter to the disciplinary sub-committee.

Rule 98 sets out what members of British Dressage shall not do, and Rule 99 deals with how a complaint of misconduct shall be made, namely in writing to the Chief Executive. If, after preliminary investigation, the Chief Executive considers that a prima facie case of misconduct exists which cannot be dealt with summarily, then the matter will be referred to the disciplinary sub-committee. (The rules do not, at present, however, set out the summary powers of the Chief Executive.)

Summary powers of the disciplinary sub-committee are set out in rule 104, and include fines of up to £50 for minor infringements of the rules, or disqualification. This is subject to the right of a member to request that the matter be referred to the disciplinary sub-committee. The chef d'équipe also has summary powers as set out in rule 105.

Once a matter is to be dealt with by the disciplinary sub-committee, the member against whom a complaint has been made will be sent:

a) Notice of the time and place of the hearing at least three weeks before the date of the hearing.

b) Details of the nature and substance of the complaint.

c) The names of any witnesses.

At the disciplinary sub-committee hearing the member may:

a) Appear in person.

b) Present oral or written evidence.

c) Call and examine witnesses.

d) Submit written evidence provided it is submitted to the disciplinary sub-committee at least three clear days before the hearing.

e) Submit written evidence and statements for consideration in the member's absence. [The rules are silent upon the time for submitting this.]

f) Request that the matter is dealt with in his absence, and may then submit written evidence and statements for consideration. This request, together with the documents, must be received by the disciplinary sub-committee at least ten clear days prior to the hearing. ['Clear days' is effectively full days: if the hearing is on the 10th of a month then it would be ten full days before, weekends not included, if abiding by the Civil Procedure Rules.]

The disciplinary sub-committee may reach a decision in the member's absence and impose a penalty. Equally, it may require a member's attendance, in which case the member must be notified that his request for a hearing in his absence has been refused no less than three clear days prior to the hearing. If a member then fails to appear after being informed that his presence is required then this will be considered a further disciplinary offence and will also be dealt with.

Members are not entitled to be represented before the disciplinary sub-committee, save that a member under eighteen years of age must be accompanied by an adult. However, a member may be accompanied by another member of British Dressage if he wishes, and the name and address of that member must be notified to the disciplinary sub-committee for their approval at least seven clear days before the hearing. There is a specific right of the disciplinary sub-committee and British Dressage to refuse the attendance of any named member whose prior approval for attendance has not been obtained.

Where the disciplinary sub-committee considers that the complaint is proven it may impose any one or more of these penalties.

1. A reprimand and caution as to future conduct. This reprimand or caution will remain upon a member's record for up to two years and may be taken into consideration if there are any further offences committed by the member within the period for which the reprimand or caution is to remain on the member's record.

2. Suspension of the member from all or any of the rights and privileges of membership for up to five years.

3. Any horse or pony owned or ridden by the member at the time of the misconduct may be debarred from competing in any competition at shows affiliated to British Dressage, to a foreign federation or to the FEI for a period not exceeding twelve months.

4. The horse or pony may also be disqualified from the result of any competition which is associated with the misconduct [i.e. if a horse has been placed in a competition at the same show and then there is an incident of misconduct, then the earlier placing may be removed, together with any points]. It is within the discretion of the disciplinary sub-committee to limit the period of disqualification for the horse or pony whilst the offending member is the owner/lessee or rider.

5. A fine at the absolute discretion of the disciplinary sub-committee.

As with the BSJA, after a conviction in a British court of law of any equestrian-related offence, a member of British Dressage may be suspended from all rights and privileges of membership pending a full investigation. The suspension has to be agreed by three members of the disciplinary sub-committee panel in writing, and may take effect from the date of conviction (rule 102a).

Under rule 103, the Chief Executive must notify, in writing, the complainant and the accused of the committee's findings and the penalties imposed. These decisions shall be binding upon all parties, subject to a right of appeal to the British Equestrian Federation under their terms of reference. Such appeal must be lodged within twenty-eight days of the decision.

Under rule 108 the disciplinary sub-committee, a chef d'équipe, or the Chief Executive may, at their discretion, publish any disciplinary decision, ruling or direction.

The British Equestrian Federation

The British Equestrian Federation (BEF) is affiliated to the *Federation Equestre Internationale* (FEI), which is the international governing body of equestrian sport. The BEF represents the sports of showjumping, eventing, dressage, horse driving trials, endurance and vaulting. It is the appellate body for all these disciplines.

The President of the British Equestrian Federation will appoint an appeal committee when required and the committee will be available to hear:

1. Any appeal from the disciplinary process of one of the member bodies or affiliated bodies, provided such body has adopted the Federation as its appellate body.
2. Any disciplinary matter referred to it directly by a member body or affiliated body.
3. Any disciplinary matter referred directly to it by the FEI.

There are full terms of reference for the British Equestrian Federation and these are found in the BSJA and British Eventing rule books.

The disciplinary procedure is as follows:

1. The appeal must be in writing, it must be signed by the appellant, his authorised agent or his solicitor, and it must state the grounds of appeal.
2. The parties must be given at least twenty-one days notice in

writing of the date, time and place of the hearing.

3. A written statement will be sent by the Chief Executive of the BEF setting out the substance of the appeal or referral.

4. A party will be entitled to be represented, or may appear in person and give oral evidence.

5. Where a party decides not to attend, rule 90.3.4 states that a written statement may be sent to the party and the matter dealt with in the party's absence. [It would appear from this that, where there is no attendance, the party is not entitled to submit any evidence on his behalf. It is not clear what the position is if there is no attendance by the party but the party is legally represented.]

6. Any party to the hearing is entitled to call expert evidence.

7. The Federation's solicitor is entitled to attend the hearing whether or not the party is legally represented.

8. Decisions will be notified in writing to the parties and the President of the BEF.

9. Where there is a penalty of suspension it will come into effect seven days after notice is given to the parties.

10. Decisions of the committee will be final and binding.

11. Costs of the hearings will be borne by the parties either in such proportions as the committee decides or otherwise equally.

12. Persons, member body or affiliated body making a referral may be required security for the costs of the hearing.

Rule 90.3.6 gives the committee a wide discretion in relation to procedures and admission of evidence subject to the rules set out above.

The committee will only interfere with the decision of a member or affiliated body (unless there are exceptional circumstances) if:

a) The finding was clearly wrong.

b) The penalty was unreasonable or excessive.

c) Conduct of the enquiry before the member body or affiliated body was unfair.

d) There is new evidence, not reasonably available at the enquiry, provided the committee is satisfied that, taken with other evidence, if the new evidence had been put before the earlier enquiry, the penalty it imposed would have been materially different.

After a hearing, the BEF may:
1. Suspend an owner, rider, trainer or other person for such period as it thinks fit.
2. Disqualify a horse from any competition or event for such time as it thinks fit.
3. Impose a fine.
4. Issue a reprimand.

These penalties will be published by the BEF and may appear in certain equestrian publications. The committee may also recommend expulsion from any or all member bodies or affiliated bodies.

Where the committee is dealing with an appeal, it may confirm or vary the decision appealed against, but cannot impose a greater penalty. The only exception to this is where the application is made by a rider and the committee is satisfied that the principal purpose of the application is to delay the coming into force of a suspension or disqualification: in those circumstances the committee may increase the period of suspension or disqualification.

INDEX